THE MIRROR OF LIFE

YOUR ADVENTURE IN SELF-DISCOVERY

BY
SHAUN DE WARREN

INTRODUCTION BY
D. E. HARDING

WELLSPRING PUBLICATIONS LIMITED
46 Cyril Mansions, Prince of Wales Drive
London SW11 4HW, England

ISBN 0 9513620 5 9

THE MIRROR OF LIFE

Illustrations including front cover: Helen Wilks
Book design and diagrams: Gill Coupland

Also from Wellspring:

By Shaun de Warren

YOU ARE THE KEY—A Guide to Self-Discovery

In collaboration with Susan Mayne and Sue Lake

THE 10-DAY BROWN RICE DIET—A Journey Towards Inner and Outer Wellbeing

Compilations

THE PROSPERITY HANDBOOK—Gems to Enrich Your Life and Pocket
THE RELATIONSHIPS HANDBOOK—Jewels to Bring Love and Happiness
THE HEALTH HANDBOOK—Pearls to Inspire Healing

For details of Shaun de Warren's other publications, tapes and workshops, please write to:

WELLSPRING PUBLICATIONS LIMITED
46 Cyril Mansions, Prince of Wales Drive
London SW11 4HW, England

By Chuck Spezzano, Ph.D.

AWAKEN THE GODS—Aphorisms to Remember the Way Home

Typeset in Great Britain by BPCC Techset Ltd, Exeter
Printed in Great Britain by BPCC Wheatons Ltd, Exeter

TABLE OF CONTENTS

ACKNOWLEDGEMENTS

My continuing thanks to Denis Vaughan, who, by recording lectures I have given in London and by making painstaking transcriptions, created the raw material of this book; to Brian Mayne who was also instrumental in providing the raw material of this book and in addition spent a great deal of time and energy in honing the text for production; to Sue Lake and Anne Green who both did invaluable work in editing the text; and to Gill Coupland for her skillful work in the design and production of the book and for drawing the diagrams.

I thank Douglas Harding for his generous introduction and Molly Parkin for the kind comments she makes on the back cover.

I continue to acknowledge all those who have inspired me and assisted me along the way, many of whom I listed in my previous book 'YOU ARE THE KEY'.

For the material in this book I would like to acknowledge additionally Werner Erhard, Satprem, Swami Shyam and Dr. Chuck Spezzano.

I am particularly indebted to Dr. Chuck Spezzano for his pioneering and empowering work on the Psychology of Vision which has been, and continues to be, of great benefit to me. I also thank him for permission to use a number of his diagrams, though I may not have presented them in the same detail as he would.

INTRODUCTION

This—I can tell you—isn't the easiest of books to write and introduction to. Attempting the task—though a privilege that's as pleasurable as it's challenging—is rather like trying to account for, and do justice to, a slice of life. A slice of existence itself, in all its complexity and subtlety and mystery. For here, in Shaun de Warren's new offering, we have a treasury of wisdom, the fruits of experience of human nature, guidance for living, compassion, shrewd counsel, warnings, encouragement—and much else. What you and I get out of it is far more a function of our receptivity than of the book's insights and meaning.

Well, I hope for better and not worse, the following is a summary of what I get, of the pattern this material falls into as I read. A thumbnail sketch of the terrain, if you like. Not exactly your map, of course. All the same, I trust that my sketch will do more to help you find your way around than to confuse you and trip you up. Please God, it may even provide something like a mini-Watership guide to the intricate system of burrows and rich grazing areas of your Warren. Anyway, here goes:

I distinguish four stages in our development:

The *first*, spanning infancy and childhood, is our apprenticeship to Homo Sapiens, so-called. Our humanising, more or less. Not to complete this stage is to risk institutional care.

The *second* is our adult life as we come to live it without any effort to make a good job of the undertaking. I mean, just the working out and putting into practice of what we have absorbed in and around our home and our school—uncritically, with very little self-awareness and less self-discipline. In fact, most of us get bogged down at this second stage, or at best somehow muddle through to the grave. We are cases of arrested development. We are the sort of people Plato had in mind when he made that rude remark about the unexamined life not being worth living.

Some of us have the luck to go on to the *third* stage. We start out on the tremendous and never-completed adventure of self-knowledge and self-direction. And, arising out of this adventure, the awesome task of taking responsibility for our interior states and their outward expression. We learn and go on learning, we hope, to the very end. We reflect as well as read. We listen when we aren't talking. We subject ourselves, however tentatively, to various disciplines. Thus we aim to realise our potentialities for effectiveness, for creativity, for loving, for having fun, and for contributing to others' enjoyment of these good things.

This is where Shaun de Warren's book comes to our aid. Every page coaxes and prods us towards this so desirable self-development, this maturation, this great work of becoming truly human. I don't need to quote examples. Just flip through a few pages, anywhere, and you'll see what I mean.

But here I have a confession to make, a problem to ventilate. It seems that, if only I were sufficiently attentive and industrious, sufficiently able to take in and put faithfully into practice this treasury of wisdom, I would indeed be truly human, and my life would work out triumphantly, and I would furnish an example to all around. Also that the dark side of me would lighten up and give me no more trouble. If only . . . . If only . . . .

Yes, sad to relate, this third stage of our maturing—needful though it certainly is—presents difficulties. To me, I mean. I can't speak for you. I run into problems, sooner rather than later. Here are just a few of them:

I have a shocking bad memory and other guides to the good life (as well as some practical experience of my own)

I have managed to stash away a goodly store of wisdom, of know-how for coping with all the nasty situations that I'm likely to come up against. For example, this infuriating friend, this wretched duty I'm resisting like hell, this ache of loneliness, or anxiety, or boredom, or whatever. Here's just the occasion when I desperately need to put my finger on precisely that wonderful recipe which matches the trouble and promises to clear it up. Alas, I've forgotten what it is and where to look it up. Or is it that I'm making damn sure that I've forgotten, so freeing myself to indulge in the old habitual anger, self-pity, bone-laziness, what-have-you? My trouble (or my excuse) is that my stock-in-trade of practical wisdom is too bulky to handle. Either the screen of my computer stays blank, or comes up with far more data than I can take in, much less act on. The result is that I find myself behaving "instinctively" after all. Which too often means foolishly, counter-productively, in my own worst interests. In short, I'm all too apt to find myself back at stage two, and up to the eyebrows in that deplorable unexamined life.

A still more serious difficulty bedevils this third stage of my life. It is that, insofar as this stage works out at all, it leaves my heart's ache unrelieved. This praiseworthy endeavor of taking myself in hand, and getting more of what I want out of life, and maturing to some degree as a human being, leaves me in the end more frustrated than ever. It's not just that these ideals of lovingness and creativity, and serenity, and courage remain very largely unrealised; but that, to the degree that they are realised, they fail to satisfy. An all-important Something is lacking. Something that transcends all human goals, achievable or unachievable.

What is this elusive Something, this Jewel that lights up the *fourth* and final stage of our life? Our true end and goal?

Shaun de Warren tells us what it is, points to it quite clearly. It goes by many names, all useful, none adequate.

It is our Source, the Mystery back of us all, our life's Root, our Reality, Essence, True Nature, Being, Who and What we really, really are when the chips are down, when all the optional extras of our life are shed.

Some folk (and I'm one of them) look to religion for a name to give This which is more ourself than ourself, which is nearer than hands and feet, which is the Hub and Centre of our life. Such as Atman-Brahman, our Buddha Nature, the Kingdom of Heaven, the Holy Spirit, the Indwelling Christ. Or simply God. I'm sure He won't mind if you jib at that name. "I don't give a damn what you call Me," I can hear Him saying, "so long as you realise that you are in Me and I am in you, eternally."

All sorts of questions pose themselves at this point. What has this fourth stage got that the others lack? Why does all that falls short of This leave a sour taste in our mouth and an ache in our heart? Exactly how does this True Identity of ours cope with the problems of our human existence? Exactly how is this fourth stage of our lives actually lived?

Let me essay, however briefly, some answers. Answers that are not for believing but for testing, for trying out.

Contrary to all rumour, Who and What you really, really are, your perfect Resource that will never let you down, is more available and obvious than all else, more handy, more on tap. All you have to do is look for It in the right place, at the right time, in the right spirit of unprejudiced openness. Thus:

You are now looking ***at*** *these words, these black marks on a light ground. All right, but what are you looking* ***out of****? What,* ***on present evidence****, is your side of these black marks? What's given, when you stop imagining things and just look? Isn't it a fact that, instead of looking out of two tiny peep-holes in a meatball, you are looking out of a single boundless Eye? In fact, out of No-thing at all? No-thing, marvellously awake to Itself as No-thing? Awake to Itself, not as* ***I am this or that****, but as plain* ***I AM****?*

Well, that's YOU! That I AM is your true Identity and Source and Resource, your deathless Reality, your Alpha and Omega, Who you really, really are.

What, you don't feel any better? You don't thrill to this divine vision? Thank God for that! He's not for feeling nice about, or thinking deep thoughts about, but for SEEING. For Seeing NOW. Right Now, in the spirit and with the same simple honesty of a little child. Utterly obvious, isn't He? Compared with Him, all else is obscurity itself.

How exactly is the fourth stage going to help me cope with the unresolved problems of the previous stages?

I have to stop pretending I am what I look like to others, and be Who I am. Which means ceasing to overlook what's right here, the Place I'm looking out from. I have to practice and get used to this essential in-seeing, and take what comes of it. And I find that, insofar as I live in the light of this central Immensity-Clarity, my human problems (which remain as many and as severe as ever) do in a sense *go away*. They don't melt into thin air, but they do obligingly push off to where they belong, out there. They belong to that fellow called Douglas Harding, to that 2nd/3rd person that my mirror and my friends and their cameras are all registering, and no longer to this First Person Singular that I AM, right here and right now. As Eckhart puts it: "God's in. I'm out." God's in. Harding's out. Praise be!

This is perfectly easy to see, not so easy to keep on seeing and living from. But this switch of Identity alone satisfies my deepest desires, because it unites me with the One and through Him with all beings forever, and with my Origin and Destiny and Timeless Perfection. Thus to be Him is to find Peace at last, to draw on the Well that never runs dry, to be led by the Guide that never fails me. To be saved is to be Him.

Off-centre now, but still real enough, is Douglas Harding, the chap who doesn't so much have problems as consist of problems. Well, what happens to that peripheral and secondary identity now that I've found my true Identity?

The great difference isn't that he's reformed or improved in any way, but that he's placed, accepted for what he inevitably is—warts and all, forgiven, made friends with, laughed at on occasions. Now that the pressure's off, and I'm no longer trying—Oh so vainly!—to polish up that fellow, there's a chance that just a little of the perfume of my True Nature may rub off onto my human nature. However that may be, this is certainly the way to live. Why is that? Because it's the way I live anyway, whether I'm aware of it or not. All of us, all the time, live from our Divinity out into our creatureliness.

What happens, then, when I'm confronted with one of those nasty problems I spoke of? *I see who has the problem.* Simultaneously I look out at the problem and in at the One Who is its solution. No need now to remember a darn thing. In fact, it's essential to jettison all that human know-how. Seeing Who I AM, I await with interest what I find myself getting up to. What that will be I can't know in advance. Of this I can be sure: it will bear the mark, the scent, the spontaneity, the appropriateness, and the authority of its Source.

The essential thing is that I discover, and keep on rediscovering, that "I am the infinite space, I am the nothingness, and I am the everythingness, that contains the Whole." Those are Shaun's words, and I can't stress them sufficiently.

D. E. Harding,
September, 1990

FOREWORD

A man on his knees prays to his God, a man with his guru seeks answers to his questions: yet where is the man who looks to himself?

I have read many books and contemplated for many hours. I have travelled the world seeking my own enlightenment and the nature of my true self, and the greatest truth I can come up with is I AM. With this awareness many sayings of the great teachers become clearer to me. Jesus' statement that "I am the way, the truth and the life" is now for me not a prescription for Christianity, nor a requirement for all people to follow the man Jesus, but rather a signpost into myself where I will find the Christ, the Buddha, the Mahanta, the source of all—the I AM. And the maxim "Man, know thyself" becomes "Man, know that you are the I AM." Again, the statement "I AM THAT" tells me that at source I AM and then I add the particular conditions of my human life out of my own consciousness and through the vehicle of mind.

No longer can I lay the blame for my life on others, nor on the government, the weather, my luck, social background, education or state of health, nor on any other circumstances outside myself. I AM and that is an end to it. I find myself responsible for all aspects of my life and, if I wish to change them, I cannot do this by simply rearranging the effects of my mental creation; I must return within myself to the awareness of I AM and transform the limiting resistant thoughts into expanding creative ones—thus from my own consciousness bringing new forms.

What is this state of I AM? It is one that is timeless—constantly in this moment—a state that is free, and has no form, is one awareness and is in the space in which all things are contained. So who I AM is who you are, who he is, and who she is. It is the one space where we all meet.

Each day we hear gloomy news about the state of the planet: the economy and unemployment; the threat of nuclear war; overcrowded prisons and mental hospitals; the threat of land shifts; and spreading pollution. Never before in human history has it been so important for man to seek his own identity to take responsibility for his own consciousness and to function from the new state of I AM. Man's technology and scientific knowledge has advanced tremendously in the last few decades, and yet man's understanding of his own Being has hardly developed at all. Most of us remain steeped in fear, intolerance, and systems of belief that separate the people of this planet into conflicting political and religious groups, each convinced of their own righteousness, yet unable to see that we are all brothers and sisters in spirit—along with the trees and cows—and that we all belong to and come from the same source. Man still seems to be working in the physical arena of security in material things, or in the mental arena of rational explanations. He appears less inclined to acknowledge his source and to work through the faculty of intuition and the Divine Presence.

But now is the time of a great spiritual awakening, and more and more people from all religious and political persuasions are making the journey within and taking responsibility for their own expansion in consciousness to that place where we all unite as one Being which is expressed in millions of different forms. If enough people can find their truth, will not all the various kinds of insanity—personal and collective—disappear from our planet?

—Shaun de Warren

THE MIRROR OF LIFE I

Ourselves in Others

Every person we know and every situation we are in is an exact reflection of our own state of consciousness.

Don't live life as if someone has the key to it.
You are the key.
Use other people only as mirrors; the true work of a guru is to mirror.
There are techniques for manifesting, but no techniques for creating, because everything is already there.
Creating is who we are.
Just create!
Create, "It's ok" and things turn out that way.

. . . If you trust life, you float.
If you fight it, you sink . . .

If something isn't working, the first place to look is in our relationships.
We look at them to heal them, and to complete all of the unfinished business in them.
To the extent that you are incomplete in any past relationships, it will show up in your present ones.
That's not very good news in a marriage.
If you are incomplete with a parent, it means you are relating with your present partner with only about 5% of your potential.
95% of you is already tied up elsewhere with incompletions with one or other of your parents, past relationships, or whoever.

This is the area we need to explore in order to unshackle it and liberate ourselves for free expression in the present.

. . . If we're having difficulties with money or health, in our creative power, or in our work, it is the same principle in action...

Dig beneath the surface and ask yourself, "What is incomplete?
What resentments do I hold?
What mind statements am I operating with?"
You can have an operating principle which sabotages any effort that you make.
You may have the operating principle, "I'm not worthy", or, "Women shouldn't be successful".
One person I know kept sabotaging everything she did.
The operating principle that she found, from her mother and grandmother, was that "Women shouldn't be successful—MEN should be successful—they're the ones who *really* know."
Every time she began to rise to the surface, she sabotaged her success at some level in herself.

. . . You may find similar analogies in your life . . .

What's going on in our thinking at all these different levels is determining what's going on in our life.
Just thinking, "I'll be successful" does not necessarily mean it's going to turn out that way *unless* I address all the statements inside that are working against it.

Dissolve the unnecessary statements.
Transform the others into positive and creative ones.

. . . This is a specific work, to clear those parts of ourselves in order that we can operate freely . . .

At a superficial level we see two people, someone here and someone there, so we're still operating at the level of duality.
In duality there's "me here" as a completely separate being, and "you there" as a completely separate being.
We feel that nothing going on in me has anything to do with what's going on in you.
Yet, in spite of this , we say, "Let's try and relate."
At that level we're still operating at a very low percentage of our capacity, like two icebergs trying to have a complete relationship using their tips only.

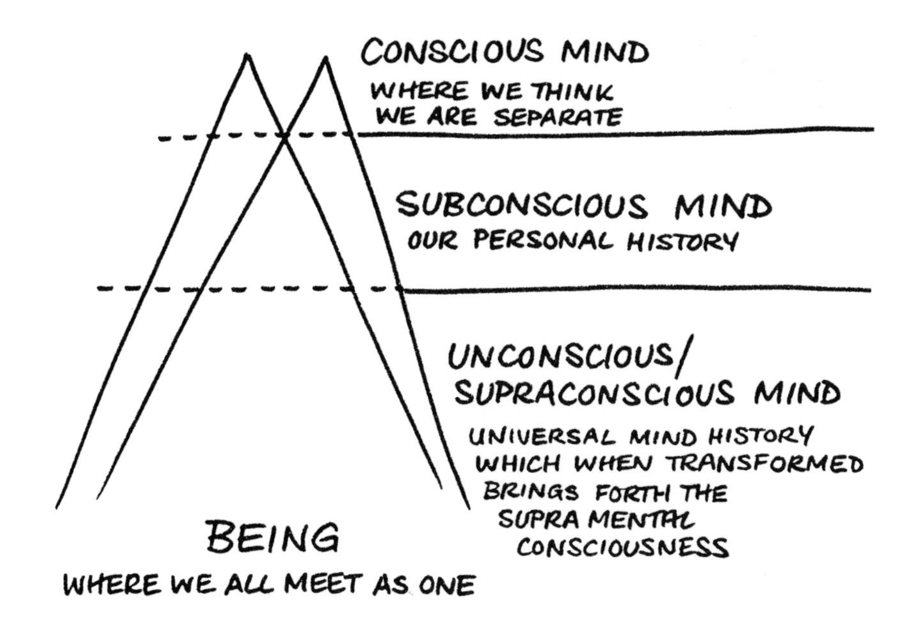

We still see someone "over there" that I've got to handle.
We see someone "over there" that I've got to deal with.
We see a "me" and a "you".
We need to get beyond this duality, and see that mind is like a sea with fish in it.

. . . These fish are thoughts.
The sea is present in all the fish.
It's just a question of which fish we are attached to as being *our* thoughts . . .

If we observe the thoughts we have, we see they are rarely, if ever, original.
They have come from somewhere else.
Our thoughts came from our parents, our upbringing, our schooling, our religion, a friend, or they've been on the planet for thousands of years.
They're just thoughts that we attach to and say, "These are mine".
These thoughts are not original.
When you recognise these thoughts are not yours, you don't have to hold on to them or defend them.

. . . What gives you ownership of thoughts in the ether?

Just suppose there's only ME, and YOU are my mirror.
This may seem an odd way of looking at things, but let's explore it.
It means going down to another level.
There is a further level below this, but let's just deal with the second level right now.

WHEN SOMETHING ISN'T WORKING IN YOUR RELATIONSHIPS

LEVEL 1. USUAL PERCEPTION: WE ARE SEPARATE
'YOU OR ME'

LEVEL 2. RELATIONSHIP WITH MYSELF: YOU ARE MY MIRROR
'YOU AND ME'

LEVEL 3. RELATIONSHIP WITH THE SELF: ALL IS CONSCIOUSNESS
'YOU ARE ME'

Suppose there's me looking into a mirror . . . a relationship with myself.
When I'm relating to you, what I'm actually doing is relating to me.
I'm seeing my reflection in you.
Everything that happens out there is reflecting me back to me.
It is telling me about my 95% beneath the surface.
I'm projecting it outwards so that I see it in you, because I can't see it in myself.
It's very difficult to see in yourself what's going on.
Once the projection is pointed out, people say, "No, no, no! That's not me! I couldn't possibly be like that!"
Yet the very fact that they operate in life the way they do shows that THAT is the way they are.

It shows in the mirror of life.

Let us suppose that there is a mirror, and that people in our life show us the mirror.
The animals, the birds and the sky are also part of the mirror, but let's just start with people.
Let us also suppose that there is *no* chance in this.
You actually select the people in your life to mirror yourself.
That is the message you are putting out.
If I'm putting out a certain message, a certain thinking, a certain set of thoughts and feelings, naturally they bounce back in the mirror.
Naturally I find myself presented with people who bounce that back to me.
This is why, if you have an operating principle, "People cheat me", you find yourself being cheated all the time.
You are attracting people who cheat you.
The mirror of life turns up the statement you are making, that "People cheat me."

It's very interesting to watch "out there" to find out about ourselves. To do that, we have to take responsibility.

Say to yourself, "I am the source of what's going on in my life."
At some level I am the source.
Obviously, I am not the source at the 5% operating level.
At some larger level of my being I am putting out messages.

I *radiate* thoughts that are bouncing back in the mirror of life so that I can see them.
I've externalised them, in order that I can see them.

We have *power* to change ourselves if we look this way.
We have *power* to recognise ourselves "over there", and then make the adjustments "over here".
The fascinating thing is, if we make our adjustments here in what we see "over there", we find that "over there" changes.
Try it and prove to yourself that it's true...

If you see a bossy, old bag over there and you've been resisting bossy, old bags all your life, recognise that what you are resisting is the bossy, old bag in you.
Honour, or acknowledge, the bossy old bag in you.
Not only does this let the other person off the hook, but you have transcended that particular problem.
It's either funny or the other person ceases to be that way for you, or it doesn't bother you any more.
Where you saw a manipulator, others may have seen a strong and powerful individual.
The perception exists entirely in you, and so does the cure.

. . . Recognise that *anything* you see in someone that bothers you, or anything that keeps showing up in other people in your life asks to be brought back to yourself, to see if it fits . . .

By acknowledging the mirror principle, "I hate him" becomes, "I hate me."
It takes courage to say of yourself the things you say or think of others.
The word courage derives from the French word "*coeur*", or heart.
The transformation is in the heart.
We can't transform ourselves in our heads.

Our heads are for information, hearts for transformation.
People think that by studying, analysing, working intellectually and having a lot of mental knowledge, they can actually make a transformation in their lives.
They say, "But I've understood all this.
I've read books on it.
I've been working with these things for years."
Why haven't they changed?
They haven't taken it to heart.
To change you must first move into your feelings and realise what's going on at a feeling level.
Take the concept and feel in your system what's going on.

. . . Once you feel it, your heart can start transforming . . .

The body is a wonderful instrument.
It helps us to discover our resistances and fears.
If we see someone and we go stiff, it is due to a reaction in the body.
We can explain it away, and invent reasons for it, but the *fact* is there's a reaction in the body, and our body doesn't lie.
We can listen to and rely on our body.
If you can think of someone, have a negative reaction in the body, and thoughts come up about this person: "They're bossy, selfish, unwilling to listen, and always right," turn that round to, "I'm talking about myself."

"I'm bossy, selfish, unwilling to listen, and always right."
If you tell the truth, you will recognise that these things *are* true about how you are, at least some of the time.
The moment you acknowledge it and say, "Yes, that is me, too", you become free of it.
You're free of being resistant to that way of being.
You let go of the other person. You let go of your judgement.

Emotional pain is resistance.
If you're in pain, you're resisting something.
Ultimately, what you're resisting is life itself, your personal process and your movement to greater expansion.
Interimly, it means you're resisting something in yourself; the shadow that you are not looking at.
Look at *all* of it, light and shadow, and own *all* of it.

. . . What I say to you, and what I think about you, is me looking at me . . .

Similarly, what you say to me is *my* invitation to you to say it.
If you tell me some things that I don't like hearing, I *listen*, because I've invited you to say those things.
If they don't hurt me, it means they are about you.
What people say about you is what they think about themselves.
If the statements touch you and hurt you, then you *look*, for it is something for you to heal.
Healing it allows you to take your next step.
This is particularly true in family relationships.
The family seems to be chosen to assist each member to grow, if they will just listen and hear.
Each has a gift for the other.

We are totally interrelated.
There is not a "me here" and a "you there".

It is very true at this level of my being that you are me.
What is going on in you is, as good, going on in me.
I cannot abdicate from what is going on in you.
This is why, when I do this healing work, what's going on in the audience or in the workshop I'm leading, the process that the people are going through, is also processing through me.
Whatever your pains and upsets are, whatever things you're working with and resolving, whatever you are trying to change in your life is, in some way, going on in me.

. . . *That* is the fundamental of healing and of transformation. There is *only* ME here . . .

The more that I can work with my state of consciousness to free it from all that which binds, the more becomes available over there.
The more that we can work together in doing this, the greater the shift in consciousness.
Healing is not something we can do *to* another person.
Many people say they heal other people.
You cannot heal another person.
Healers actually heal themselves and the other person gets better.
Healers create the space in which the other person can heal himself.
The healing process happens within.
It happens from the Oneness.
It happens from your relationship with yourself.
The more that we can work together in doing this, the greater the shift in consciousness and the greater the healing throughout the world.

. . . The transformation that takes place on the planet starts with the individual . . .

We are looking into the mirror of life.
Everything that's happening in my life is a direct reflection.
If there's something I'm trying to change, or something that isn't working, there's no confusion about it.
I can see how it reflects in other people.

The other side of the mirror of life is that the beauty, the joy and the love you see in other people is also in yourself.
If you see loving people, acknowledge that it's a loving person looking.
If you see prosperous people, joyful people, happy people, then that is who is looking.

It's intelligent for us to start looking this way.
See the beauty in people.
See people as divine beings, as expressions of love.
Don't see them as the negative things we think and say about them, as that is a reflection on us.
It not only describes us, but binds us to that way of thinking.
Criticising people actually holds us in misery.
You have the choice of being righteous about how wrong people are, or you can be happy.

. . . You can let the whole thing go and be happy . . .

I was talking to a man whose wife had left him after 35 years of marriage.
He was terribly upset about it, and focused on the "badness" of it.
He thought it had destroyed his life.
I said to him, "Just suppose you set it up that way.
Suppose at some level you really wanted her to leave."
He thought about that and responded, "Two years ago, I couldn't have accepted such a statement. Looking at it now I can see the marriage was getting a bit stale. The truth is, I did want to move on."
The truth was that he had really created this change.
Within the mirror of life, he had set up a situation where he was set free, and, of course, so was his wife.

As soon as he acknowledged to himself that he had caused the separation, all the blame he placed on his wife disappeared.
Both were free to take their next steps.
If there truly is love there, they would come back together again.
In the intervening two years he had expanded so much, studied so much, and discovered so much about the inner world and different levels of being, that he said, "There's no way I would have looked into all this, if that hadn't happened to me."
At some level in his being there had been a stirring, and it brought about changes for him.
It wasn't at the 5% level, as at that level he still wanted to hold onto this woman.

By holding on to the past, as if you shouldn't change, you are in pain.
. . . And yet, *you* bring the change.
You arrange it . . .

Let go of the past.
Allow the present to express itself, so your future is the much more evolved future that is laid out for you.
You cannot have the evolved future if you stay operating from the 5% level.
You move beyond that.
If you find that you're resisting, that you're in pain about something, it could be that you're holding on to the past.
The Self, your divine spark, or divine aspect, has only your good in mind, and wants you to move forward.
It wants you to move to that which is truly for you, to your special place, your special expression in life.
It's been working for this for years, probably lifetimes, if you accept reincarnation.

It's this new child within, this flower in your garden, that is working to express itself as you.
Each flower is different.
We don't all have to be daisies, or dandelions, or lupins.
In order for the new to emerge, the old has to break down.
At first it may appear as though something's going wrong.
Up in the 5%, the tip of the iceberg, it looks as if it's all falling apart, as if something's not as it should be.
It's more like I need to check my relationships, and find what I'm holding on to.
I need to look into the mirror of life, and see what it's reflecting back at me, to get the messages.

. . . When we begin to work at this level, everything comes to our aid . . .

Nothing is excluded.
I am dwelling in this Oneness.
I am recognising the Oneness in everything.

. . . Everything participates and becomes a part of It . . .

Everything in the universe reflects consciousness.
Nothing is separate from it.
Two examples of this happened during a recent seminar.
At a very heavy moment in the seminar, when there was a lot of resistance to these ideas, the electric fire exploded into flames.
Looking at the fire, I said, "We've created a lot of resistance to what's happening here."
Everybody saw the joke, because that's what it was.
In that moment the resistance shifted.
Everybody laughed and the atmosphere lightened.
Later, when I was presenting an opportunity to shift and move from formbound thinking, "I am this body" to, "I am this space", the door of the room flew open.
Someone said, "What's that?"
I said, "What do you think?
The door's just opened
You have a chance!"

. . . Now is the time to take that step, to let go of your formbound thinking and to move into Being . . .

Let go of past thinking.
Be the space.
When we're the space, we start looking in vision.
We become visionaries.
When we express and have everything we see in vision, a fundamental shift takes place.

We cannot reason it.
We cannot work towards it.
It just happens.
It's stepping out of the thinking "I am this form and this thinking."
I step out and see thoughts like fishes swimming past.
I observe the emotions in this body system.
I see this body, and I am the space that contains it.
It's simple.
There's nothing mystical or difficult about it.

. . . It's stepping backwards and observing. In the moment we do that, we realise there's only One. There can only be One . . .

Surrender the search for "me" and be the Looker.
What observes, what perceives, what sees, is the real Me looking.
It is the mental glasses we look through which distort the world we look at.
It is the glasses we correct.
I am seeing myself.
That's the mirror of life.

The truth is that when you see or have problems, you are restricting your own expression.
It's *always* restriction, because who you *are* is sublimely, divinely beautiful, free, expressive, loving and wonderful.

. . . The reason we're unshackling this is so you can truly be *you*. It opens you to something more wonderful than you had . . .

THE MIRROR OF LIFE II

The Spiral of Life

The more I can transform my own reality, the more my world changes, both in the way I perceive it and in the way I live it.

Miracles start to happen.
As everything is interrelated, a healing "here" leads to a healing "there".
By changing the subliminal messages you put out, the "outside", as represented by other people, changes.
A partner who rejects you is responding at some level to your messages.
Making your partners wrong and trying to change them does not work.
Addressing your inner fears and resistances brings the change.

. . . It is by addressing your own fear of rejection that you bring about the change . . .

We all have certain addictions.

We think they're "over there", but they're here, and unless we transform them they get closer.

Each of us is in the centre of our Spiral of Life, with the family in the first circle, followed by close relationships, and, as it radiates further out into the world, the Spiral finally includes everybody and everything, everywhere.

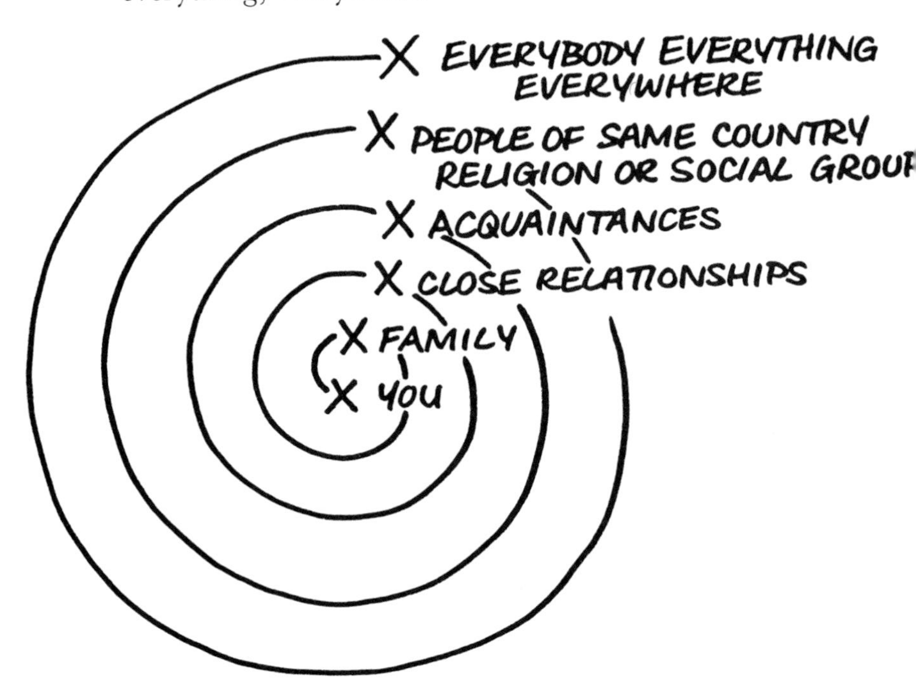

You may have a particular negative thinking or dis-ease.
If you heal this condition, the healing reaches out through the Spiral, beginning with family, and eventually reaching the whole world.
Whatever you resolve in your life, will start moving out in the universe in this spiral of interrelatedness.

. . . It will go out further and further . . .

The Spiral of Life also works the other way.
If someone out there on the Spiral has got some life-threatening condition such as AIDS, cancer, heart dis-ease, or starvation and you are not working to resolve it, that condition starts moving closer to you on your Spiral.

. . . The conditions exist within the Spiral of your own consciousness. By working to heal your own life, people with such conditions are served by your actions and the condition need not close in on you . . .

We cannot abdicate our responsibility for what's going on within the Spiral of Consciousness.
If someone is starving over there, unless we start taking action to eliminate starvation in our own consciousness, as well as taking appropriate physical actions, it's going to start moving in.
One day someone you know is going to be starving, and then someone in your family is going to be starving.
At some level *I'm* starving.
My starvation may be for love; someone else's may be for food.
If I address my starvation for love, I will find that there will be a change in my environment and in my thinking.
This will start radiating out and those people who don't get food suddenly do.

People show up who start resolving the problem.
We may also choose to go and give people food.
This is work for some of us, but not all.
The major work is to define in what way we are starving, and to start resolving our own hunger; then we can listen to what is appropriate in *our* life.

. . . By taking responsibility as the healer and resolving what is going on within us, we can in turn make our contribution outwards to all on the planet. Each of us can play our part . . .

Who I *am* is responsible.
Who I *think* I am is not.
Responsibility is not shouldering the blame or the load.
Responsibility is a quality of being.
I am naturally responsible and so are you.
The mental structure, being immersed in belief systems, is not responsible.
Thoughts heal nothing.
Whatever has been thought or said has never made any difference.

. . . What brings the transformation is the quality of Being. Quality of Being is Who you are . . .

The whole of the spiritual work is recognising who you *are* and transforming who you think you are.

Who I think I am is this mess of things: "I'm good at this, bad at that, I came from here, I'm going there, these are my parents, that is my past..." none of which is responsible or competent.
You raise yourself to Being and natural responsibility.
As you open up into your responsibility, you do what's appropriate for you, what you like to do, and what you feel good about.
It is natural and spontaneous, not something you feel forced to do.

. . . In responsibility there is no "I ought to", "I should", or "I must." There's only the spontaneous doing of what you do—what you *love* to do, *want* to do, and *choose* to do . . .

In cleaning up the unfinished business of the past, your future changes.
In resolving your relationships, and returning them to love, your future changes.
In dropping the past, you also drop the future and live in the present.

. . . After all, what *are* the past and future? Just a tape recording in your head. On realising this, you step free of them . . .

At a global level, only a few years ago, people were thinking that we would be lucky if we could stagger into the next century.
Now, everything looks much brighter.
What happened?
Some past thinking was transformed.
This meant that a new future will open.
By creating a peaceful, prosperous future and by inviting others to align with that vision, that future becomes a possibility.

We are not our past.
Who *we are* is who *we are*.
If you think you are your thoughts and your body, *the form*, the past is important to you.
Once you discover that you are the Divine Being, the past becomes an interesting story, but no longer holds you.

Fear is the last enemy.
The way to address fear is with vision.
Vision transforms fear.
If we live in the condition of a warring world, we're in fear.
If we live in the vision of a peaceful world, we transform the fear we have.
It's in vision that love from the heart transforms the condition.
In a global sense, we are transforming the condition of life.

The power of vision is that it's a here and now experience.
We can only have vision here and now.
Everybody is potentially a visionary.
We can look in our vision and see a wonderful life, a happy relationship, and success.
It is our attachment to past thinking that gets in the way and says, "No. You can't have it that way, for such and such reasons."

Instead of putting other people down in order to feel better, we will find that they lift us when we acknowledge them.
It is a massive power for healing.
They raise us so we can live this life triumphantly, and so can they.
We are all interconnected.
At the level of being we are all one.
We cannot really separate ourselves from anyone on the planet.

If you start resolving from love, you become a little sun, a little bundle of love.

You start resolving your life, returning it to love, giving up your attitudes about your family and the closest people around you.

You find that your love goes out and you start resolving global issues.

. . . The love generated from you goes outwards and outwards, till people many spirals away from you start receiving the benefit . . .

THE MIRROR OF LIFE III

Roles

A role is something we play out to separate ourselves from others.

If I give someone the role of dependence, it must mean I've given myself the role of independence.
The effect this has is that I cannot receive.
If I play the role of the "helper", I will allow no-one to help me.
If I play the role of the "expert", I will listen to no-one's wisdom.

. . . If I play the role of the "spiritually advanced one", I will allow no-one to show me the way. In my "betterness" I separate myself. . .

Why do I play a role?
As I cast myself in the "helper" role, is it that I feel helpless?
I want to feel important, the other side of feeling helpless, which is a helping-to-*get*, not a helping-to-*give*.

True helping is something else altogether.

True helping is natural leadership, a giving of ourselves.
The gift we receive is in the giving.
It comes spontaneously out of our being and has nothing to do with playing a role.
In separateness I always compensate by trying to present the other side of what I feel.
I will probably find my actual feeling is the exact reverse of what I am projecting.
If I feel weak, I act in an aggressive way.
Aggressive people are people who feel insecure.
If they felt secure, why would they be aggressive?

. . . People who shout and scream are actually saying "Help! I need attention. Please love me." When you know that, you don't react. You respond with love . . .

When playing the expert, you are covering up your ignorance.
You want to feel important, and you feel important when you appear to know it all.
You think the role will win you the approval of others.
What it actually does is to create a barrier to your receiving and a constant stress; like being the fastest gun in the West, you live in fear that someone knows more than you do.
When you're playing a role with anything, *you* don't receive, only the role receives.
You yourself are starving.

. . . The role gets all of the acknowledgement, the thanks, and the love—and you get nothing . . .

As I play the role of the "spiritually advanced one" it is a plaster casing over my feeling of inadequacy.
In my attempt to persuade people that I am better than them, I hope they will love me.

What actually happens is that, even if they do, I cannot feel it.

A duty is what I "must", "should", "ought to" do.
Duties are performed in burden and sacrifice.
There is no love or joy in them.

. . . The very same things we can do, not as duties, but as our gift of love. In that moment we receive our gift also . . .

STEPS TO PROSPERITY

Prosperity is a state of Being.
It is not a "thing".

We tend to think of prosperity in terms of notes and coins
. . . and let our bank accounts determine our level of
prosperity.
This is not the case.
Take the example of an apple tree.
Sometimes there are apples, sometimes there are not.

. . . As long as the tree is alive, however, it is
"apple-prosperous". Apple trees, by their very nature
are "apple-prosperous" . . .

Human beings are prosperous in all the ways necessary for their fulfilment and satisfaction.
Problems arise when we find we have barriers to our true expression of prosperity.
These barriers, in the main, are emotional and mental resistances to expressing our natural and inherent wealth.

Money is only a symbol of prosperity.

STEPS TO TAKE TO RELEASE AND EXPRESS OUR PROSPERITY:

1. Align with prosperity consciousness

Create: "I am prosperity itself."
"I think prosperous thoughts."
"I feel prosperous."
"I see prosperity."
"I have wealth."
"I do what wealthy people do."
"I am grateful."

2. Find your operating negatives or limited thinking patterns and turn them into positive openings

(a) First consider all the attitudes about money held by those important to you in your formative years, including your parents, grandparents, teachers and church.

Here are some examples of attitudes held:

"Money is scarce."
"I must work hard to earn money."
"I shouldn't have money."
"It's selfish to have money."
"Spiritual people should be poor."
"Money is the root of all evil."
"Money is hard to get."
"You can only earn money if you've got a proper job."
"You have to be brilliant to earn money."
"Getting money easily is cheating."
"I can't have love *and* money."
"If I have it others will have to go without."
"Money is vulgar."

"Women shouldn't earn money."
"More than enough to survive is greedy."

Think back and add your own list additional to these. Perhaps:

"I don't deserve wealth."
"People cheat me."
"People with lots of money have got their priorities confused."
"I always end up without money."
"I can't hold on to money."
"If I spend money, I have less of it."
"I can never create enough."
"If everything turns out, I'll have to die."

When you've listed all the negatives that you find in your thinking, you can recognise them as your limiting operating principles with regard to money.
These principles will determine the condition of money in your life.
No matter how hard you want it to be different, it will always be this way until you transform your thinking.

(b) Now take each operating principle and turn it into a positive creative statement:

"I can't make money" becomes, "Making money for me is easy."
"Money is the root of all evil" becomes, "Money is a blessing from which all can benefit."
"I don't deserve wealth" becomes, "I deserve and enjoy my prosperity."
"If I spend money I have less of it" becomes, "When I spend money I express and share my prosperity."

"Making money is hard work" becomes,
"Prosperity is my natural state, so creating money is easy for me and any work I do is for my expression and enjoyment."

3. Start building these new statements into your consciousness

Write them in a book or somewhere you can refer to them regularly.
Whenever you catch yourself thinking or operating from one of your old statements, take time consciously to build the new statement as the reality for you.
This you can do by sitting quietly, thinking and feeling the new statement, and repeating it to yourself until new energy is released as the mind accepts the truth of it.
You may have to do this many times until the old statement is replaced.
A system of fining yourself is a good technique.
Every time you catch yourself with one of your old statements, place a pound (or any sum you choose) into a box which must then be spent on having fun at the end of a given period (a week or a month).

4. Recognise that money is a love energy

(a) See money as a love energy, rather than a thing.
Giving and receiving money is similar to giving and receiving love.

(b) Learn to realise that supply is not limited, only demand for it is limited.
Train yourself to make demands on your consciousness, to be creative in making money.

Set yourself projects that you're enthusiastic about.
That stimulate the mind to come up with the creative ideas and means that will generate the supply.
This is more effective than simple money targets, which the mind often has difficulty in accepting and therefore is not willing to play flat out.

(c) Be open to all the channels through which your supply can come.
Do not limit it to your present accepted income(s).
Be willing to open to your creativity.

(d) Do what you love doing and love what you do.
Doing anything else is a waste of time and not your most creative way of expressing your prosperity.

5. See creating money as a game

It is not necessary to be so serious about money or business. It is simply a game to play. The only question is whether you play it badly or well.
Since money is a necessary commodity on the planet, at this time, it is intelligent to become effective players of the money game. Create goods and services that are of value. The game is won when we have enough money to do what we want with our lives, either when we're clear of the need to work for money, or when our present level of money creation satisfies our needs without burden.
It is not necessary to play it forever.
There are plenty of other things to do.
Play the game so that everybody wins.
Recognising and manifesting prosperity is an enjoyable adventure—and lots of fun!

6. Clean out

(a) Forgive everyone for everything they have or haven't done, including yourself.

(b) Make a list of all people who need your forgiveness and consciously release all your attitudes about them.
Discover what gifts you have received from their being a part of your life.
Transform the relationship you have with them by moving from "victim" to a grateful receiver of gifts.

(c) Clear out the clutter in your life: possessions, unneeded things in the house, cupboards, drawers, car, handbag, briefcase, etc.
Prosperity has difficulty manifesting in a cluttered consciousness.

7. Take responsibility for being your own paymaster

(a) You alone know your own worth.
People will only pay you what you are willing to receive.
Recognise your self-worth and build your self-esteem.
Self-esteem is developed by acknowledging who you ARE: Divine Being and *already* prosperous.

(b) Be responsible with your money.
If you aren't, no-one else will be either.

(c) Manage effectively what you have.
Give up worrying about what you don't have.

8. Practice giving and receiving

Money is a circulation.
Learn to circulate it lovingly, generously and easily.
Give money to those who inspire you.
Be willing to receive gifts of money.
Tithing and seeding are common practices and can be explored by those who wish.
Tithing is giving one-tenth of what you've received to your church, organisations or individuals who inspire you.
Seeding is giving one-tenth of what you wish to receive: if you wish to have a £1,000 holiday, donate £100 towards someone's holiday and await your harvest in the same way a farmer does.
All giving is unconditional and given with love.

9. Practice acknowledgement

Acknowledge the people around you who are prosperous.
Align your consciousness with theirs.
In acknowledging others, we acknowledge and awaken those qualities in ourselves.
Allow yourself to receive compliments and acknowledgement.
Allow others to tell you about the talents and positive qualities that they see in you.
The problems we have hide our gifts and talents.
The "problem" is helping us reveal those very talents by making us pay attention and seek the gift hidden in it. Put these talents to work. Share the gifts you have with others.

10. Relax and give up the struggle

Struggling against the enemy poverty only brings more poverty.
What we put our attention on increases.
Relax.
Take it easy.
Create in your vision what you want and *ask* for it. Apply the principles of manifestation*:

VISION:	Visualise in as much detail as possible what you want as reality.
CLARIFICATION:	Clarify, or focus, your vision.
DECLARATION:	Commit, intend, for your vision to happen.
PREPARATION:	Prepare, clear the space, for it.
ACTION:	Take action, starting in small, appropriate, ways.

11. Get started!

Start now!
Tomorrow doesn't exist.
You may not know how to do it yet.
Just start and find out as you go.
Start from where you are now.
Create the vision of what you want.
Move towards it.

12. Step by Step

Hold the vision of your ultimate goal but take small steps in achieving it.

*[See also The Laws of Manifestion chapter in YOU ARE THE KEY—A Guide to Self-Discovery.]

Thus each step becomes a victory, building your confidence and self-esteem.

BE PROSPEROUS

Prosperity is a state of consciousness within which you know that the calls you make on supply are always met.

I lived on the shady side of the road and watched my neighbours' gardens across the way revelling in the sunshine.
I felt I was poor and went from door to door with my hunger.
The more they gave me from their careless abundance, the more I became aware of my beggar's bowl.
Till one morning I awoke from my sleep at the sudden opening of my door, and you came and asked for alms.
In despair I broke the lid of my chest open and was startled into finding my own wealth.

—*Rabindranath Tagore*

INDIVIDUAL SOVEREIGNTY

We are all individual expressions of the Deity.

Each of us is individual and has a vital part to play in the creation of the planet, even if we don't see it that way yet.

Life is an adventure in consciousness, and a joy—or nothing.
You choose.
We are sovereign in our own life.

... So far, most of us feel that we are the effect of life, that in some way life is doing it to us, and we are not the cause ...

We often live in the drama of life.
We have a good story to tell, and explain it.

It is time that we changed things in our lives.
Why put up with things the way they are?
Why is there suffering, disappointment and misery?
Is it meant to be that way?

It is unthinkable that God would create a place from where everyone wanted to escape.

We are often conditioned to think that this is the bad place, and the good place is elsewhere.
A lot of yogis and religions say: "Suffer here, so you can go to Heaven, which is over there ... another place."
They say Heaven is good, the world is bad.
I say the world is good. Let's build Heaven here...there is no other place.

In our drama we see our lives being controlled by external forces.

"I didn't have the right start in life."
"I didn't get the right opportunities."
"I'm not pretty enough."
"I'm not young enough."
"I'm not good enough."
"I just have bad luck."
"It's my stars."
"Mummy wouldn't like it."
"Daddy wanted me to be a lawyer."
"I can't go out without a scarf on, or I get a cold."
Does cold cause colds?

We are trained to look outwards—to see the world outside of us.

. . . We think the outside forces control us, whereas it is our subconscious thinking which determines the way we experience life . . .

Some people are upset by anything; they are like a walking "upset machine".
It's time to be sovereign in our lives.

Positive thinking tries to deny the negative.
It says, "Think positive!"
When you stop thinking positive, the negative gets you; it comes in and wipes you off your feet.
While you are in duality, trying to resist the negative brings more negative.
If you fight the devil, you get more devil!

Positive thinking doesn't mean you've dealt with the negative—all you've done is avoid it.
The negative is a part of the creative process.
Without it there's no transformation.
There can't be oneness within which there is only one pole.
So with "positive thinking" you exclude the negative, rather than embrace and include it.
Good/bad, right/wrong, disease/health are all aspects of consciousness.

. . . Since consciousness comes from God, then it must follow that *everything* is good! By taking responsibility, we include all of it. We don't deny the bad, or escape it. We transform and integrate it . . .

The individual is the most powerful thing there is in terms of the power of *being*.
We all have the power to be, to create, to generate a whole new life for ourselves and others.
Let us acknowledge this power and use it.
The great saviours of the past knew about it.
Instead of trying to dominate each other, we take a step into consciousness.
Let us elevate our thinking from separateness into oneness, into an awareness of a pure state of consciousness ... an energy.

Matter is energy asleep.
If I awaken this energy, it begins to change form.
If I heat ice, it melts and changes form.
In consciousness we can change matter.
In consciousness we have the power to change the condition of our health, and of our lives and relationships.

. . . We can't change anything by applying thinking to it, anymore than a television can change its own programme . . .

Our thoughts are like a massive computer attached to emotions.
Sit still in quietness or meditation, and watch the mind programmes that are controlling us.
Be aware of them, be aware of the mind statements..
Sit still in the centre of your being and observe the patterns.
In stillness we can see what runs our lives.
We see that at the centre of our being we are whole—not halves.
From wholeness we can see how we limit ourselves.

Once I've recognised my wholeness I will recognise your wholeness.
Then we can share as two wholes.

Avoid looking for completion of ourselves in other people.
You can't be sovereign in your life if you see yourself as only half a person.

Our completion is found in ourselves.
You are a whole person, complete, perfect and immortal.
Perhaps your presentation is not yet this, but *you* are.

. . . As you return within to your essence, you find it is true, you contain all . . .

I contain all and you contain all.
I can't separate any part of the world from me.
The body expands to a universal body.

Feel the reality of it.
Who said that we end at our skins?
Can't you feel the presence of people far away?
We all have experiences of telepathy.

When people die, they go everywhere; everybody is further enriched by them.
They change their form, but they have not gone away.

See people in terms of a presence, then it doesn't matter if they're somewhere else.
Their essence lives on in your heart and in all people, when you recognise that their essence is love.
You may lose one loved one, but when you recognise that the loved one lives in your heart, you see that love shining in many people.
You seem to have lost one, but you have gained billions.
Love knows no distance, no time, no form.
Love cannot be separated.
It simply is.

. . . We are not limited to the physical boundaries of our bodies and functioning. Maybe it is only belief which stops us from being able to see and hear at distances, to communicate across dimensions and time . . .

Be the generator of your own being.
Let go of belief in external healing practices.
Use them, but abandon the belief that they are going to do it without your participation.
You generate your own health.

Generate your own money.
Let go of the belief that someone will always fund you.
It is most disempowering to find out that the whole world is controlling you, because you don't have any money.
To reclaim our sovereignty, we must be able to generate our own goods and services and be the source of our own money.
See yourself as the creator of your own income.

Be the source of your own relationships.
Open yourself to receiving.
Let go of the expectation that others should make you happy.
We create our own satisfaction and our own joy.
We create them out of being, because we can see them in our vision, not our condition,

. . . We create "All is good—life is good" We are thus beginning to live as a visionary. I'm the source, and I'm the sovereign in my life . . .

If I believe in my word, it becomes law.
As I speak, so it shall be.
We have the power of the word, if we say it with authority.

We created the world the way it is, which means that we've created war, disease, cancer.

How did I create that?
Through pure ignorance. Through not knowing that I am a creative, conscious being.

Avoiding doing it is as bad as doing the wrong thing.
Participate in life in such a way that the conditions which we see are spiritualised.

We are shifting into a future which is created out of consciousness, not out of mind.
Each becomes a conscious being.
Each stands in his or her own right as equal sovereign beings.
We generate our own lives and work in partnership with each other to bring about a new way of being.

It is not a new way of doing it the old way.
It is a new level of being, which we must take, or our planet may be destroyed.

. . . The starting place is to be the source of our own lives. Reclaiming our own sovereignty. Use only those mindsets which are useful. Create prosperity for all people. Live from that state of being and transform yourself until you achieve mastery and beyond . . .

THE NATURE OF BEING I

Discovering the Formless

We're enquiring here into the nature of being.
We are all explorers in this adventure together.

If we go to another country, we get the roadmaps and we orientate ourselves easily.
The roadmap for the journey within is not so clear.
Some Indian literature has mapped part of the journey, from a spiritual view.
Westerners are now mapping the journey from a psychological view.

. . . As Western and Eastern maps come together the road becomes clearer . . .

It is exciting for me that we are ALL mapping as we go.
We are on the road together.
We share the things we discover with each other.
Together we move into different dimensions of reality.
Together we understand being more fully.

At present we are moving into an age of partnership, an age of interdependence.
Everyone is beginning to work for the benefit of the whole.
There is less working against each other, climbing on each others' backs, and being "the hero".
We're all leaders in the coming age.

. . . The time has passed for just one or two divine beings. The "Second Coming" comes in all of us . . .

Being has no boundaries, frontiers or form.
It just Is.
It is brought from the formless into the formed.
That formlessness is all of us.
The initial step we take is the step from the form to space.
In letting go of the idea "I am form", we take this step.
Formbound thinking says, "This body, these thoughts and emotions are me. Everything else is outside of me. I, as a "me", must find my place in this vast universe."
This thinking leads to misery.

. . . The step into space returns us to ease and creativity . . .

The misery of formbound thinking comes as we try to "fit in".
We make strenuous efforts to acquire things, so that this "me" looks successful in the world.

We become vacuum cleaners, sucking into ourselves the things we think we need—prestige, acknowledgement, titles, position, money and power.
By doing this, we think that happiness and satisfaction will follow.
When we "have" all the things we find they do not.
It is then that people ask the question, "What the hell's life all about? Years of struggle are leading me nowhere!"

. . . It is then we discover the way of acquisition is a cul-de-sac . . .

Let us take the fundamental step from "I am this form" to "I AM".
When the truth of this sinks in, we realise we are not a part of anything.
We are the whole within which everything moves, lives and has its being.
Suddenly, WHO we are becomes the Space within which the form exists.

Be the Space in a room.
Notice other bodies also exist in the Space.
Notice that "I" seem to be expressing as one of the bodies.
From where you look it appears that someone else is speaking.
At a body level this is true.
At the level of being, where only One exists, "I" speaks as this body and as all bodies.
When you speak, I also speak.

. . . "I" is not attached to any particular form, but speaks as all forms . . .

When we take this step we find that everything that we ever want or need or dream about already exists right here and now.

In the state of I AM everything already exists in potential.
It is not a question of acquiring it.
It is a question of expressing it.
It is a "FORM-alising" it, and a willingness to receive it.

Life changes from "getting" all sorts of things for this little particle "me", to recognising the fullness of Being.
We are already whole, complete and perfect.
Rather than takers, we become givers.
In giving we receive.

. . . We cannot receive unless we can give. We cannot give unless we can receive. Inherent in the gift is the receipt . . .

As we become givers, we become "give-uppers".
We let go of those things which we've been holding onto.
We surrender attitudes, attachments and beliefs which limit us. Our personal "sadhana", or work on ourselves, is to bring us to a fullness of being while here in the physical domain.

The extent to which this shift takes place is the extent to which we recognise the Oneness which exists.
As we go deeper within, from layer to layer in the exploration of who we are, we find more and more of our wholeness.
As our wholeness emerges, we become aware that there can only be pure consciousness ... the One Self.

All separation disappears.
You and me disappear into "I".
Our separation only exists at the level of the physical.

...With our two eyes we divide. Where the eye is single there is only one...

Where the eye is single there is Vision.
In Vision there is creativity and love.
In Vision we find that all those mental and emotional things we are holding on to, all our misery, our pain, our fear, our doubts and confusions, are attempts to hold on to our physical world positions, which can just as well be released.
As the Watcher we can see them spread out in front of us.
We stand free of them and, in this freedom, can begin the process of letting them go and returning them to the Space.

...In the giving up, nothing is lost and everything is gained...

In acknowledging our Beingness we are enabled to forgive and let go.

...When we let go, we are spontaneously aligned with being. We find ourselves in a wellspring of love and vision...

THE NATURE OF BEING II

Transforming the Barriers to Being

The barriers, whatever we resist or find so difficult, show up in the mirror as whatever it is that we won't acknowledge in ourselves.
Once we acknowledge them it's over.

If I'm terrified you're going to find out that I've got, say, a big nose, I say, "Have you noticed my big nose?"
You say, "Yes, lovely," and it's all over.
Otherwise, all during our conversation the thought "Has she noticed my nose yet?" is in the way.
With an underlying operating principle of, "I'm no good" the barrier to communication is, "Have they discovered I'm no good yet?"
Or "Have they discovered I'm unlovable?"
Or "Have they discovered I should be rejected?"
These things go on in the 95% of us that is beneath the surface.
They're not in the surface 5%.
These thoughts and feelings come up for us as we interact with others.
Be alert to them.
Observe them.

... Alertness is meditation. Notice these things "as if" you're watching them. YOU are watching them ...

When the thought comes up, "That person's really arrogant", I now observe, "Aha! I've got a thought 'that person's arrogant', I have acknowledged the arrogance in my thinking."
The moment you notice the perceptions are in your own thinking, you can release the other person.
When your attitude is, "That person is domineering", you notice the thought "that person is domineering", and can observe the role you play of being the dominated one.
In surrendering this thinking our attitude about the other person is transformed.
You can be grateful that he helped to show you the game you are playing, even if it was unbeknown to him.
It enables you to free yourself.
When we see Divine Being only, we are acknowledging our *own* divinity.

. . . When we see anything less than Divine Being, that's what we need to resolve in our own lives. The acid test is, "What do I see 'over there'?" . . .

Loneliness, for example, is a separation.
It's a fear of participation.
By participating and sharing ourselves, loneliness disappears.
"Aloneness" is "ALL ONE-ness".

When we are truly "alone", we are truly "ALL ONE".
Often people seek to distance themselves from this world and look for their "oneness" as being some other place, some other heaven.
It was not God's intention to make this place so that we must escape from it.
This is heaven!

. . . If you don't like this place, transform it with love and creativity. Trying to escape it does not work. Our Heaven is here . . .

At source everyone is a divine, loving being.
All are included.
If I'm Divine Love, so then are you.
By seeing you as love, I invite that response.
If I relate to what I think are your flaws, I invite that reaction.
If I present myself as the flaws that I think I am, I invite you to treat me accordingly.
This is not something we work out in half an hour.

. . . People have been working for clarity of being for years and still find plenty more to do. It wouldn't be any fun if it were easy . . .

In making a commitment to self-discovery, our barriers to being come up.

If we commit to freedom, our barriers to freedom come up.
If we commit to love, up come our barriers to love.
Commitment brings up the barriers.
It also brings up the opportunity to dissolve and transform.
In India they speak of *vrittis* and *samskaras*.
Vrittis are the little thoughts that control us, like, for example, "Oh, I must have some chocolate."
They are little things in mind that bind us, but are not seriously damaging.
A *samskara* is a major emotional scar, a major incompletion.
Samskaras can be created by the death of a loved one, physical assault, rape, accidents, major failures, loss of liberty, torture and loss of limbs, or other deep emotional shocks.
Samskaras can also be inherited through the family (family karma) or brought through from other lives, including from such things as sudden and painful death.

These can bring up operating principles such as:
"No-one loves me."
"All men are bastards."
"This world's a threatening place."
"Life is unfair."
"The world's against me."
"It's hopeless." or,
"I can't succeed."

The resultant life conditions of these statements keep turning up in life until they are cleared.
Once you recognise the *samskara*, and are willing to release the destructive judgement you have made, you're on the way to its healing.
If you don't acknowledge the *samskara*, you think the world really is that way.
You'll say, "Of course, all men are bastards. Can't you see?"

You'll give us plenty of evidence to prove it.
"Every man I get involved with is like that," you'll say.
Naturally, since your invitation to men is, "Be a bastard," they respond accordingly.

. . . It is better to notice, "I have something to heal around my relationships. Perhaps I should consider my relationship with my father, mother, grandparents, brother, sister, or other major relationships in my life—good or traumatic—and see what needs to heal in me" . . .

It helps to have the assistance of someone who understands the process in clearing *samskaras.*
It helps to work in a group.
Have someone who is an open space for you and can ask the right questions.
Choose to be in a group of spiritual beings working for their spiritual freedom.
It is in the everyday situations that we really find the opportunity for working on ourselves.

. . . But in everyday life, should you say, "I'm feeling *really* upset," the normal response is, "There, there. Never mind." rather than "What's going on in your system that seeks to clear itself?" . . .

When you look from Oneness everything becomes a gift and is for your benefit.
Aggression towards you gives you the opportunity to recognise your own aggression and to be free of it.
When you're aggressive towards one person, you're aggressive towards the universe, and that aggression adds to the pain of all people.
The invitation to be aggressive does not come from being.
It comes from our thinking.

There's who we *are* and there's who we *think* we are.
It's who we *think* we are that creates the drama.
"You are wrong," or, "Please beat me up," are thoughts.
By looking from where we are and who we are, we can observe the who we *think* we are.
By being still inside you can watch the thoughts and emotions coming up.

. . . You can ask the question, "What happened in my past that I should think and feel this way?" The answer to this question is the beginning of the solution . . .

The starting place is willingness.
When you're willing to forgive another, the opportunity presents itself.
If you're unwilling to forgive another, the same situation keeps repeating itself.
To hold on is crazy.
It is an attack on yourself.
Your anger invites attack and your negative energy returns ... with interest.

. . . That which you fear is brought upon you. That which you fear for your children is brought towards them. The greater gift is to let go of the fear and trust . . .

We're a radio station.
We're just broadcasting whatever we're putting out all the time.

We can't fake it.
We can't go around just saying "All is goodwill and love" and expect the universe to respond to our words.
The response is in accordance to what is genuine in our hearts.
The heart is the organ of transformation.
The mind is for learning and storing information ... it does not *change* anything.
With information we can understand it all, even write books about it, but nothing *changes*, unless our heart is in it.

. . . It takes true forgiveness, a giving up of all my attitudes about you in such a way that I feel love towards you—love that brings a true healing, a transformation . . .

Being is the true healer and pours into the world of form to heal.
Another word for this is love.
It is the love that you generate from being into the world that transforms the condition.
Healing is local and universal.

In working to heal one body, you work to heal all bodies at some level, including the planetary body.
If you work at a planetary level, the benefits must also show up at a local level.
You can't separate the one from the other.
In holding negative energy about a single person, you hold yourself from love and you hold yourself apart from the world.
You hold it in separation from yourself and from everyone.
This is craziness.
It takes energy and effort to maintain ill will against another person.

. . . Constantly holding a grudge is hard work! Why not use the energy for creative activity? . . .

Being of itself is inert, neutral—neither positive nor negative, but containing both.
Love, health, and power are generated from being.
It's not enough just to repeat,
"I think I'll be powerful."
"I'm powerful."
"I'm a very powerful person."
"I'm a very powerful, loving, healthy, prosperous person."
"I'm a powerful, loving, healthy, prosperous person.
"My life works and everybody loves me."

We must bring being to it.
Give it life!
Affirmations only work when empowered with our being.
In generating love, all the barriers to love come up for clearing.
If, when generating love, a judgement comes up about you and I notice I make you wrong, I am the only person who can release that judgement.
You may spend your whole life trying to make it up to me, but there's nothing you can do, because I've erected this wall called, "You're wrong".

. . . In my willingness to generate love, I find the opportunity to release my attitudes and move towards my personal freedom . . .

We make who we *think* we are right and this makes the other person wrong.
When there is right and wrong, conflict starts and love is lost.
We have the choice to be right or to be happy.

Guilt occurs when we have done one thing and we think we should have done another.
We make one right and the other wrong.
Guilt is what we put in the middle, so that we can retain both thoughts and not resolve the issue.
For example, "I should be visiting my mother, but I'm here."
Guilt holds the two in place and I can continue to be here and not visit my mother, so long as I am guilty enough.
With guilt I can tolerate two separate positions which are inconsistent.
If I take out the guilt, I am left with choosing either to be here or going to visit my Mother.
Guilt for something done in the past is a way of avoiding healing the situation, such as doing what it takes to make amends, including self-forgiveness.
Then what happened becomes history.
It ceases to burn inside.

. . . Life is a wonderful opportunity to live fully, lovingly and excitingly right NOW. Why drag along this great sack of stuff from the past? We can let it go, just like that . . .

Every thought is a past thought.
Once we have a thought, it is past.
History is thoughts we've had.
Once we recognise it's the thoughts we have had that bind us, then we observe the thoughts and simply let them pass, like fish in the sea.
The thoughts we have had tell us who we are *not.*
Knowing who we are *not* is very liberating.

"I'm right."
"I'm wrong."
"I'm guilty."

"I'm to blame."
"I'm upset."
"I'm the hero."
"I'm the villain."

. . . are all thoughts that we've had.
They are not who we *are*, simply a drama we create.
Who I *am* is innocent pure being. The rest I made up.

. . . This is the rebirth of the Spirit, the recognition that
who I *am* is pure love, pure being, pure awareness . . .

LIFESCRIPTING

A fortuneteller can predict your future.
You're the only one who can change it.

Why do we always write about the past as if it is solid and real, and about the future as if it is yet to come?

Who said the past has gone and the future is yet to happen?
Do they not both lie in our consciousness now?
The past we have already scripted.
We can just as well script the future, as we have the past.
When we script the past it appears to us as solid and definite.
This past we call, "The Story of My Life".
Notice, however, who did the scripting.
Notice who are the heroes and who are the villains.
What was good and what was bad.
Notice this in our script.

. . . Should our thinking be transformed, "The Story of My Life" would sound entirely different. So even our history loses its solidity . . .

The future most people give themselves is based on their interpretation of the past.
A gloomy view of the past leads to a gloomy view of the future.
Or we live in wild dreams which, deep down, we know will never turn out.

. . . Yet we live in their pretence and use these wild dreams as an avoidance of reality and of our responsibility to transform the present . . .

When we realise that both the past and future are merely tape recordings in our heads, we can train ourselves to script a future that is nourishing and creative.
We can script the future by looking into the vision of what we want and writing a script of how it will happen, as if it is happening right now.
Lifescripting is a *now* event and we live it in our thinking and feeling.
In our vision the result is already achieved.

. . . The script reads like a diary and gives the events and experiences that brought about the result. It is like a filmscript with words and pictures . . .

When writing our script, it is important to ensure that we are not writing anything that is detrimental to, or in any way manipulating, others.
Nor do we write into our scripts any others without their permission.
"George and I are getting married" is not a script we would write without George's permission.
"I now have the chairman's job" becomes, "I have the perfect job for me".
This gives the chairman the freedom to be in the perfect place for him without me trying to steal his job.

. . . My perfect job may be somewhere else that I hadn't thought of. When I think and feel the perfect job for me, it may feel similar to his, but it is not "his" job. Mine shows up in its own way . . .

The way we're thinking now and the thoughts we've had about our past *will* determine our future unless we change them.
If we have this limiting thought about ourself in any area, *that's* what's going to turn up in the future.
We get more of the same.
We get more of what's happening now and what has happened in the past.

. . . When we take responsibility for shifting some things in our thinking and feeling, then it will turn up differently.

Expectation leads to misery.
In expecting, or manipulating, something to turn out a certain way, we are inviting pain, because it probably won't.

Lifescripting is a form of creative writing.
What we write may turn out entirely different from what we set out to do.

The gift is that what turns out is appropriate and what we need.
Everything becomes a gift.
If a relationship falls apart, you lose your job, you become sick, whatever happens, there's a gift.
Look for the gift.
There's always a gift, whatever happens.
Don't put your attention on the problem.
Whatever you put your attention on increases.

The art is in creating how we intend it to turn out, without being attached to the result.

When scripting, be open for the miraculous.
There may be openings for you in the future that you have not yet thought of.
Allow space in your script for these possibilities.

We tend to think that a miracle is something that happens "miraculously".

... A miracle only happens with a changed state of consciousness. It does not happen by itself alone. As we let go of our limited thinking, and open to the miraculous, it has a way of turning up ...

Whatever you can do
or dream you can,
begin it.
Boldness has genius,
power and magic in it.
Begin it now.

—Goethe

THE POWER OF ACKNOWLEDGEMENT

The only person that you can ever acknowledge is yourself, as there is only One.
In acknowledging other people, we are really only acknowledging ourselves.

If you say to someone "You're a very loving person", you are acknowledging the love in yourself.

. . . Develop acknowledging as a way of life . . .

People are starving for acknowledgement, not for what they've done, but for who they *are*.
We've been trained to put people down, to defend ourselves and make ourselves look good.
To acknowledge others—ourselves—is to overcome our shortcomings.
We open ourselves to our Self.
It becomes a powerful vehicle for returning everything to love.
If you acknowledge someone for something, it completes and creates space for new relationship.

. . . Until we create space there is no room . . .

We can acknowledge people ALL the time.
Look for what you can acknowledge.
It is a powerful way of lifting others and, as you lift others, you lift yourself.
Use every opportunity.

. . . Acknowledge in others that which you wish to bring forward in your life. If you wish to improve your health, acknowledge the healthy. If you wish to have money, acknowledge the rich. If you wish to have a life partner, acknowledge those who have partners and loving relationships . . .

Acknowledgement can be especially powerful when it is especially difficult to do:
There was a man who hated bankers, because he thought his father had been ripped off by them.
He was out of work and had no money, because his attitude against bankers separated him from his wealth and his natural career.
His healing assignment was to stand in the City, outside the main banks, and acknowledge every banker for his wealth and integrity as an honourable human being.
He did not know how to do this, but agreed reluctantly to give it a try.
After several days he got into the swing of it and began to enjoy it.
The healing had begun.
It wasn't too long before he was happily employed—in a bank.

. . . Start an acknowledgement programme. "I am responsible for what happens in the world. So we can take responsibility personally for acknowledging the world" . . .

There are many ways we can acknowledge.
With words, "I find you 'loving', 'humorous', 'organised'."

With money—love in action—as an expression of acknowledgement, we can reverse a sense of scarcity.
Money is the most physically demonstrable commodity to show us how life works, a wonderful tool in learning to master the rest.
Write letters to acknowledge people for what they're doing.
Sometimes just one letter can make all the difference in someone's life.
It may be that no-one has truly acknowledged them before.

. . . Acknowledgement works wonders, even when it doesn't come from whom it was expected . . .

If you feel unacknowledged, ask for the acknowledgement you want.
Don't sit in suffering saying, "No one acknowledges me!"
An acknowledgement out of the blue can give a great lift.

. . . When you acknowledge, acknowledge from the heart; making it up for effect can be counterproductive . . .

Some people find receiving acknowledgement difficult.
This is only because they have low self-esteem.
Just keep acknowledging them.
Being unwilling to receive acknowledgement is as limiting as not giving it.

To acknowledge yourself is to accept that you have all the natural qualities of Being.
The German greeting "Grüss Gott" stems from, "The God in me greets the God in you."
Acknowledging yourself means acknowledging the God in you, the Self in you.

. . . Once you raise your self-esteem with this principle, you no longer need to put others down in order to shine . . .

Acknowledge people to other people.
Raise people in the eyes of others.
In this way we raise the level of the world a little.

. . . Become the acknowledger. People feel good that way, and people feel good about us . . .

Pay bills with acknowledgement and love.
One lady who thanked the gas board learned later that her letter was circulated to every employee in the company.
Everyone needs acknowledgement, including the gas board and the tax office.

. . . Pay bills with love and gratitude and acknowledge the providers of the service. Sometimes it may not seem easy, but look for a way to acknowledge them . . .

A friend told me that a book of aphorisms which I had written some years ago always helped her whenever she needed inspiration or guidance.
It has also helped many of her friends.
I felt acknowledged by that.
By looking at what that experience was to me, I found that it returned me to my creativity.

. . . I felt that the acknowledgement seemed to be a completion of something and an opening . . .

What is the dynamic of acknowledgement?
For me it is returning the thinking we have about something to the source.

Let's use the symbol of a circle.
Who I Am, Love, God, is outside of the circle.
It is All and Everything, Nothing, the Space, the Essence, the Source.
I am All, Everything, Nothing, Space, Essence and Source.
So Space, the context of life, is outside the circle.
The inside of the circle represents the form.

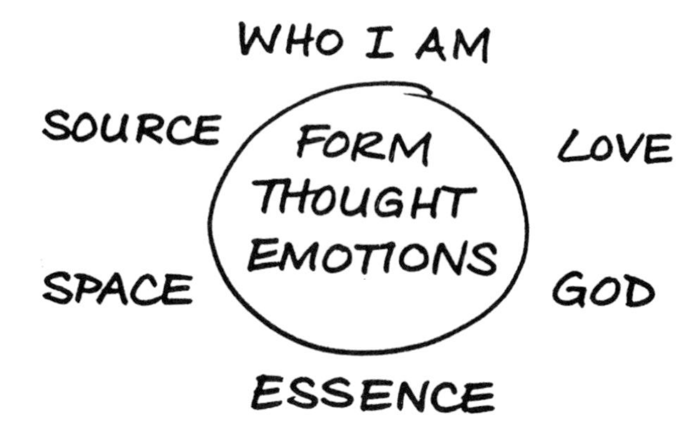

When we look from the Space into the life we lead, we see the form that is there.
Most people are sitting in life and form trying to find the Space.
This is trying to manage cause from effect.

Most people I know think they are formbound reality.
People think, "I am a form".
They think, "This body is me.
I have to identify this body with the rest of the world.
That's my relationship.
What this body doesn't have is what I don't have.
What it lacks is what I lack.
What this body needs is what I need.
I must go out and manipulate the world in some way in order to get to me what I lack."

The trouble with this formbound thinking is that it is also problem thinking.
If I don't have it, then I've got a problem.
I see that my solution is over there somewhere.
I have thinking which says that I don't have it.
"I don't have it and I want it", creates a feeling of lack and pain.
Acknowledgement is returning to the source the thinking we have had.
All thoughts are in the past.
Every new thought is already gone as soon as we have had it.
Every thought stays within the circle.

... If I return thoughts I have had to the source, I let go of that set of thoughts. All feeling of ownership of those thoughts disappears along with their corresponding restraints ...

This letting go of attitudes is easily seen in the acknowledgement of people in relationships.
We see it as forgiveness.
If there are problems between two people, normal thinking is, "I've got to do something to you to make you understand it my way".

Or, “I’ve got to fix you up in some way so that the problem is solved”.
At best, “I have to forgive you” in this model of thinking is not true forgiveness, as you and I remain separate in duality
The good me is forgiving the bad you.
We still have a “good me” forgiving a “bad you”.
Forgiveness is returning the thinking to the Source.
So, forgiveness is an acknowledgement.

... If I let go of my attitude about you, and acknowledge your source, which is the same as mine, then the problem is solved, because there is no problem ...

To begin acknowledgement, we must understand who we *are*.
Go back to the key: Who I AM.
It is the key to everything, as you may have noticed.
The trouble with talking about “who I am” is that any label brings it into the circle.
If you say, “Who I am is infinite space” then you become an “infinite space form”.
You cannot explain “Who I AM”.

Explanations are forms, and bring an indefinable feeling back into the mind.
IT IS, and there’s an end to it.
The only way to get to who I am is to identify, “Who I am *not*.”

I'm not the clothes I'm wearing.
So, I'm not the thoughts I've had, the feelings I've had, or this body I'm wearing.

. . . I'm living in this mass of thoughts as if it's here. We have to be able to lift that off, just like the clothes we wear, and what we're left with is Who We Are . . .

By noticing the thoughts we are having and by *being with* them, we are able to return them to the Source.
We do this by releasing our attachment to them.

. . . We now surrender the corresponding emotions and actions induced by them . . .

When we acknowledge the Source, creativity is present.
We become empowered.
When acknowledgement is present, we are ready to give more of ourselves.

In interpersonal relationships, if I *know* that this is who I Am and what is going on is going on, and I know that you are the same, and what's going on with you is going on with you, what's going on with you has nothing to do with me and what's going on with me has nothing to do with you.
It is just what is going on.
If *that's* the case, I don't need to make you wrong any more.
I don't try to manipulate you into my viewpoint any more.
What's the point?
Who I Am is who I am!
Why should I try to get you involved with my viewpoint, which is inside the circle of formbound thinking?
By releasing,
"I think you're wrong",
"I think you shouldn't have done that",

"I think you could have done it a different way", or whatever I'm thinking, and the feelings of upset and hurt and all that follow my thinking, if I can allow it to be happening, and know that who I AM is who I AM, and who YOU ARE is who YOU ARE, I can actually separate myself and see what's going on.

If you know Who you are, and you use acknowledgement, your past begins to clear.
You can see all the thinking of your past coming up for you to look at.
All your incompletions with your mother, your father, your schooling and your church all come up for you to deal with, when you acknowledge who you are.
You can deal with it, because what is a lie dissolves, when you adopt the process of BEING WITH IT.
The lie disappears in the space of Being.
All things that are false are transitory.
All resistances to Being will disappear.

By taking responsibility for what's going on with you, and not blaming someone for it, you are able to clear it.
By clearing it, you return to your God Self, your Creative Self, your Free Self.
That is the key to dealing with interpersonal relationships of all sorts.

When you acknowledge another person, you are actually saying, "I, the love self, recognise you, the love self", "I see you as divine being", "I, the godself, recognise you, the godself."
You are no longer a problem, a stranger, or someone I have to deal with or handle.
I acknowledge that you are a divine being, and I notice that there is something going on in me, about you.
But I recognise that whatever is going on in me about you really has nothing to do with you.

. . . Now, if there's something going on in you about me, that's what we need to hear and resolve by returning it to the Self . . .

Another attitude we might have is, "Everybody in the world is a stranger to me".
I was on a plane and thought, "Look at all these strangers here".
Then I thought, "If I return that thought to the source, and acknowledge that Who I AM is Who they are, they are no longer strangers.
They are my friends, brothers and sisters, fellow travellers, divine beings ..."
In that moment, I had a different sensation: "Oh! Look at these wonderful people!
I wonder how I am, looking like that?
I wonder how I feel looking eighty years old?
I wonder how I feel looking ten years old?
I wonder how I feel as the pilot?"
There was a shift in the way that I perceived these people.

. . . It was as if Who I am is in the room in as many forms as there are here.

My main interest in getting into a relationship with you would be to find how I am as you.
So I've returned it to the Oneness.
I'm One with you.
That is available to everybody.
You just do it.

. . . Simply acknowledge the Oneness—that there is only One—only one anything . . .

The same principle applies in everything we do.
It is returning from dual, formbound thinking, into the One Thinking.

Take relationships:
In acknowledging others, we acknowledge ourselves.
In acknowledging others, we free ourselves.
I've had very strong experiences of feeling bound to people, or to organisations, in my past, because in some part of me I had not acknowledged them.
As soon as I acknowledged them with "You have been a contribution in my life", I was immediately free.
Whenever you feel that someone or something is binding you, acknowledge them.
You return the binding thoughts to the Source.
"I recognise you as Divine Being.
I recognise myself as Divine Being.
I surrender any thoughts that I have about you that bind.
I generate goodwill and love for you and I set you free."
We may not use these exact words, but this is the sense of it.
If you feel bound to any person, whether by positive thoughts (such as hero worship), or negative thoughts (such as greed, envy and upset), it means that you have not acknowledged them in this sense.
We know our acknowledgement is completed when we feel that release and change from within.

. . . By acknowledging many things in my past, I became free of all of them . . .

By acknowledging the great spiritual teachers, such as Jesus Christ, Mohammed, Buddha and Krishna, we raise ourselves out of the binding and limiting dogmas into the essence and the light.
In that instant we are free of all the formbound structures of religions and yet at the very heart from which they flow.
When we acknowledge something it is complete.

. . . By acknowledging each moment, each day, as a divine gift, we transform the past and are free to live creatively in the present . . .

The whole principle of spiritual healing is to acknowledge the source of healing.
If you feel unwell, be aware that "Who I AM" is fine, and "who I THINK I am" is having an experience of feeling unwell.
This is a clear distinction.
The unwellness is in your feelings, and it is to your feelings that the healing is brought.
Thinking is holding you from the acknowledgement and experience of health.
When the source of health is acknowledged, the possibility of feeling well returns, you are reconnected with the divine energy and it flows naturally into all levels of our being.
A real therapist just puts people in touch with their creativity; and when your attention is on that, rather than on the problem, the problem vanishes.

. . . It is the creativity, the love, that heals . . .

A way to health is to directly acknowledge "I am the source of health".
See the health in other people and align with that health.

It is like saying, "I acknowledge that you are an extremely healthy and vital person and I know that vitality exists as much in me as in you.
I now call that same health and vitality to express myself."
It is difficult for people in hospital to get well as there is little health to acknowledge and align with.

. . . If you put sick people with healthy people, they can begin to acknowledge health and to feel healthy...

The same with money.
Hang around with people who haven't got any and we'll get none.

. . . The way to have money is to acknowledge the people who are prosperous, and find out how they do it. The same is available to you . . .

A list of things which will not get you what you want includes:
—worrying about it,
—bitching about it,
—making people wrong about it,
—or saying "Oh God, please give me what I want".
None of these work.
This thinking is not going to get it, because there is no acknowledgement in it.
We separate ourselves from the good we want.
The more we strive to get the things we think we haven't got, the more we separate ourselves from them.

We live our lives as if there is one more piece of the jigsaw to be found.
There isn't.
There are no more pieces of the jigsaw in that thinking system.
That thinking system says, "Everything that I want, I don't have".

. . . I say, "Everything that you want, you have already".
Just acknowledge having it and acknowledge those
who have got it. There is the power . . .

Heal the "twoness" thinking, the separation from the
things that we want.
Forgiveness and gratitude are two of the greatest messages
in the Bible.
Forgiveness means returning to the source.
Give up your attitudes *about* something.
Gratitude, the great attitude is
"Thank you.
I acknowledge the source,
I am the source,
I have everything I could possibly want,
Thank you."

By acknowledging that we already have what we want, we
open the door to expressing it in form.
Time lives in the circle.
When you acknowledge something, in that moment it exists.
The task is then to bring it into physical reality.
If you're sick say, "Thank you for health".
If you're lonely say, "Thank you for friends".
If you feel unloved say, "Thank you for love".
If you feel poor say, "Thank you for wealth and
prosperity".

. . . By aligning with what we want at the level of Being,
we open the door to its manifestation . . .

Envy closes the heart in the chakra system.
Acknowledgement opens the heart.

. . . Acknowledgement returns you to the source of your
wellbeing, to the source of all those things which you
wish to express in life . . .

Acknowledge people for the contribution they make to your life.
Speak to them, telephone them, or write to them.
If someone on the radio, television, or a lecturer inspires you, or you read an article or book that inspires you, write and acknowledge that person.

. . . Thank them for the gift of what they're doing. This empowers them and it empowers you . . .

Acknowledge someone with whom you disagree, even though they think your thinking is "wrong", or you think their thinking is "wrong".
You know that all that has happened is that you have different thinking patterns.
It is not that they are wrong.
By allowing them to think what they think and to do what they're doing, they feel acknowledged and you feel good.
Acknowledgement comes as a gift of recognition that they are whole, free beings.

. . . Other people's existence does not depend on the way you think, nor yours on theirs . . .

Each one of us is the Whole of us.
Take responsibility for being a source for Being.
Who we are matters, and each of us is a sourceful, powerful being, when we choose to be that way.

. . . The more you acknowledge others, the more you are acknowledged . . .

LAUGHTER, THE VOICE OF THE SOUL

It is natural to laugh.
Life is light, joyful and easy.

. . . *Or we make it heavy.*

We make it heavy by being serious and significant.
We burden ourselves with the trappings of mind.
By freeing ourselves of these burdens, laughter returns,
Enlightenment is lightening up.

. . . We become lighter.
And the light shines . . .

It is impossible to dislike someone who makes us laugh.

. . . We love people who make us laugh.
People we make laugh love us . . .

Laughter is a great healer.
By laughing we release stress and negative emotions.
When we laugh over 400 secretions are sent from the brain through the body.

The Chinese monks knew this and laughed for half an hour every morning.

. . . Laughter is infectious.
It is something we catch . . .

To laugh with another person we must drop all our attitudes about that person.
We cannot hold on to our attitudes and laugh freely.
Laughter is one of the quickest ways of healing relationships.
It is worth practising laughter until it is spontaneous.

. . . It is no wonder that comedians are the highest paid people, and the most loved.
With laughter what a wonderful world this is! . . .

MY EXCITING LIFE

No one else is living your life.
It is uniquely yours.

Each thing you do, each moment you live, is unique and never happens again.
We can make these unique moments exciting for others by identifying their fun and joy and making that experience available to them.

. . . By being enthusiastic about our lives and the things that we do, however humdrum they may seem, others are lifted . . .

Enthusiasm, from *Theos*—God—"to fill with God", is something we generate from our wellspring.
Of itself it is inert, and is brought into being by us.
We become the fountain of enthusiasm.
Observe the people who write about their lives, lives probably no different in essence to yours or mine.
Yet they write and speak of them in a way that inspires and amuses.
By being enthusiastic about our lives, others become enthusiastic about theirs.

By seeing the uniqueness in our friends and the people around us, we invite them to express that uniqueness.

To make our lives interesting and exciting we charge them with Beingness.
We bring our very Selves into everything we do.

. . . Life becomes a game, like a party where everything is new and everything is fresh, even things we've done many times before . . .

Look for the unusual.
Look for the things we can share with others that inspire and uplift.
Let go of the hard luck stories,
Let go of all desire to engage people in negative agreements, such as how bad people are and how bad the world is.

. . . The world is the way we make it . . .

Choose to create a world that is a joy to live in.
Seek to discover new awarenesses in the fields in which you're interested.
Share these discoveries.

. . . Do the things you really want to do.
We are only alive when we are doing what we want to do . . .

...Take risks.
Risks are exciting . . .

...Have courage.
Courage strengthens us and transforms the quality of life . . .

...Think big.
Thinking big is exciting for others . . .

...Live life as a personal laboratory,
An opportunity to discover and grow . . .

It is not what we DO that is necessarily exciting.
It is WHO we are that is exciting.
Each of us is exciting when we know WHO we are.

Therefore . . .

. . . Be unreasonable.
. . . Reach for new horizons.
. . . Open new spaces.

. . . Seek not to compare your growth with the growth of others.

Seek to be more fully yourSelf today than you were yesterday . . .

...Say, "My life is exciting."
Be *willing* for it to be that way . . .

SEX

It is natural to be sexual.
Suppressing sex does not lead to enlightenment.

Celibacy cannot be forced.
It happens naturally at the right time, for the very few.
Celibacy is a state of Being far more than it is an act.
Having sex is a loving, joyful recreation.
It is a sharing of energies, a balancing.
It leads each participant to a higher level of Being.

. . . It is a doorway to the experience of Heaven . . .

We often think of sex as an act, starting with foreplay and ending with orgasm.
Men often see it as a performance, something they 'do' to a woman.
They tend to think that sex is a way to expend energy, and that that is its function—a release.

. . . A far deeper level of sex is communion, being with each other in loving embrace, touching, sharing . . .

. . . Women seem more aware that sex, in its purest form, is
being together.
To be truly in the moment together, united, ONE . . .

...Sex is naturally fun, so that we are able to engage in it
in order for the species to be recreated.
If sex were not fun, the species would die out . . .

Many people seek love in sex, moving from partner to
partner in search of love.
Seek rather to bring love to sex.
In that way it is always fresh and new with the partner
you have.
For love sees only love.

. . . Often just cuddling and lying together, Intimacy and
tenderness
Is all that is wanted . . .

Having sex with a person brings with it a blending of
certain psychic energies.
That person has an influence on our auras at several levels.

. . . That is why it is intelligent to choose our sexual
partners carefully.
Choose partners who enhance our energy, not
debilitate it . . .

It is OK to feel sexual towards people other than our
partners.
Denying our sexual feelings creates resentment towards our
partner.
By acknowledging our sexual feelings and moving towards
them with integrity,
And without betraying any agreements we have made with
our partners,

We find that all our relationships are enhanced.
By moving towards someone we feel sexually attracted to,
we move through various levels:

—Sexual attraction
—Friendship and love
—Recognition and acknowledgement of their Essence
—Transcendence and transformation

Once we have reached transcendence with one person,
A transcendence beyond our sensory limitations,
We have opened the opportunity to reach the same
transcendence with everyone.

This is taking sex out of the act and into the realm of BEING,
Where twoness becomes one
And all separation,
With its allied pain,
Disappears . . .

As you acknowledge the attraction in others, you
acknowledge that quality in yourself,
And it becomes a gift to your partner.
The very qualities we found attractive begin to show up
and radiate in our partner, since there is no
separation.
Repressing your feeling of attraction towards another, or
their feelings of attraction towards you, shows up as a
lessening of your attraction towards your partner and
vice versa.
Love suppressed turns to anger and resentment.
Grant your partner the freedom to be attractive and
attracted to others.
The gifts all come to you.

. . . Whatever qualities we acknowledge in another person,
without being drawn into an inappropriate

relationship with that individual, those same qualities are available to us, and surprisingly show up in our partner . . .

Everyone who wishes to have a sexual relationship should allow themselves to.
When choosing a partner, ensure that they are free and willing to have a sexual relationship with you.
It is impossible to have a sexual relationship with someone who is not truly available without involving the other's partner.
If such situations occur, it is important to complete the relationship with all people concerned.

. . . Completion is a bringing to wholeness, not an ending . . .

Sex is an energy and the very vital force of our Being.
People were being sexual long before the churches were ever thought of.
There are many attempts to deny sexuality, or to deny it in an unnatural way.

. . . When we acknowledge our Being as Love Itself,
We recognise we are like the sun,
All there is to do is shine . . .

The partner we have, becomes everyone of that sex for us.
If our partner is male, he represents all 'Men' for us, contained in that body.
If female, she represents all 'Women' for us, contained in that body.

. . . When we truly know who they are
They are Love Itself . . .

TRANSCENDENCE VERSUS TRANSFORMATION

Traditionally spiritual seekers have always been trying to transcend, to get out of this reality into higher states.

The attitude has been that the physical world is 'evil', 'lesser', or the 'dustbin of the universe' and that what we must do is get out of it.
Most religious and spiritual practices came from this thinking.
Heaven became a place in some other reality, beyond the grave.

. . . Churches' heaven is somewhere else.
You have to wait until you die and then you might get a ticket there—or you might go to the other place . . .

There is no above and below.
They're the same.
It is a circle.
Heaven exists 'down here' just as much as 'up there'.
It's all the same.
We reach up and down.
Reach down into life.

Take life on.
Include life, rather than exclude it.
People isolate themselves trying their best to exclude everything.
"If I can exclude everything, cut out everything, and be totally still, then I'll find Nirvana, heaven, or whatever IT is."
We cannot find God by excluding everything.
Everything is God.

. . . The key is to include everything and acknowledge our freedom in it . . .

Heaven and hell are dual thinking.
Dual thinking belongs in the mind.
There is a reality which contains all duality.
In each aspect of duality dwells its opposite.
In hell there is heaven.
In up there is down.
In out there is in.

People looking for their inner reality often limit it to the space contained by their body.
They exclude the rest of the universe in their search for the 'inner'.
Include the seemingly 'out there' ... all the other bodies, sounds and sights.
There is only here and now.

. . . *This* is Heaven and hell.
There is no separation in either space or time . . .

Once you shift awareness, 'in' includes 'out there'.
Our outer reality becomes our inner reality.
Everything is included in our inner reality.
Our inner reality is nothing and everything.
The inner and outer come together and are the same.

Many yogis reach for Nirvana, a total withdrawal from this world into a state of bliss.
Often this is a cul-de-sac.
Transcendence is getting out of this reality—trying to maintain some 'other' reality.

. . . But when you come back from your transcendental experience, this reality hasn't changed at all.
We still have our relationship difficulties.
We still cannot pay the bills . . .

We cannot separate reality.
It is all here.
This reality is all there is, therefore this is the reality that must change, or nothing changes.

. . . Thus from our transcendence we must also descend and transform . . .

All the drug-takers and people who use various techniques to transcend the body get peace and bliss momentarily, but it's not enough.
We need to transform.

. . . To transform means to bring Heaven here, so that this reality changes.
The present conditions in our lives and on the planet give way to more elevated ones . . .

Transformation is a two-way journey.
Go up and bring your transcendent experience into form.
Transform so that the condition changes here.
We think the condition here is solid.
We think there is nothing we can do to change the essence of our lives or relationships, except by bashing the form around.
In fact, everything is 99% space.
There is very little matter in this planet.
If we look at something with a powerful enough microscope, all we see is space.

. . . We can awaken matter to its true spiritual nature, and life changes . . .

A fundamental shift which will bring a transformation into life is:

"I've lived all my life as if I were form.
Now, I live my life as Being, or Space.
I notice the form is within my Space."

Now, suddenly, there's nowhere to go, nothing to do, no Heaven to reach for, no evil to fight.

. . . All that is left is to bring consciousness into the unconscious and raise it to the light . . .

If our relationship with money changes in such a way that money seems to happen in our life, that is a transformation.
It is a shift in consciousness, not something we've simply 'handled'.
If warfare ceases, it is a transformation.
'Handling' war simply suppresses it for a time.
Peace is not the absence of war.
It is the creative state, peace.
We cannot get rid of war by studying war.

We cannot get rich by studying poverty.
We cannot get well by studying sickness.
Studying cancer does not in itself end cancer.
Something more is needed.

. . . When we bring true awareness to the conditions of life—disease, war, poverty, misery—a transformation occurs and the condition disappears from the face of the earth . . .

The starting place is in the lives of each of us.
Everything that happens is an opportunity to discover our ability to transform.
We are the transformers and our bodies are the instruments of transformation.
The work is done through *this* reality, through the body, through matter.
Instead of getting out of the conditions we don't like, we are mastering the ability to transform them.

. . . We transform hell into Heaven.
Heaven is a space, not a form . . .

Bring the space of Heaven to the form earth.
This is transformation.

We bring health here, so that disease disappears.
We bring peace here, so that war disappears.
We bring love here, so that pain disappears.
By ending our own hunger, hunger ends on the planet for all.

. . . We bring all of the qualities of Being here and make fundamental changes in our environment . . .

The macrocosm and the microcosm reflect each other.
The planet is a living entity, just as we are, not a football.

We cannot kick it around, pollute it, and abuse it and still
expect it to function any more than we could expect
our own body to function when mistreated.

. . . The planetary body is our body.
It is not separate . . .

...Transformation is the most important work we can engage
in.
It is the high road to discovering the possibilities of "What's
next?" . . .

BE GOOD TO YOURSELF

Often we are generous with other people and totally mean to ourselves.

We are happy to give gifts and compliments.
We give money, often to our own disadvantage.
We consider ourselves generous.
And yet we are mean with ourselves.
We are mean in that we do not allow ourselves the riches of Heaven.
We seldom give ourselves gifts.
We do not go out and spend money on ourselves . . . simply for the joy of spending money on ourselves and having the good things.

. . . Somehow we feel it is wrong that we nourish ourselves . . .

We slog hard in life to achieve.
We have goals to achieve,
Success to achieve.

. . . We have to get somewhere.
All we get is stress, disease and unhappiness . . .

We are mean to ourselves with acknowledgements and compliments.
"I'm a failure."
"I'm not good enough."
"I'm boring."
"Others will disapprove."
We punish ourselves with shoulds, ought to's, guilts and fears.
We do this until our life becomes unbearable.
Still we think the only way out is to try harder.
In our moments of insight we look back to the times of our life in which we experienced some happiness.
In those moments we were free, loving, in touch with ourselves and at ease.
In such moments we are aware that 'important positions'
And what men call 'success' are not the happy moments.

The happy moments were walking on a beach
Reading a book
Looking into someone's eyes
Sitting in a cafe
Talking
And laughing
Being with friends.

. . . We realise that the essence of happiness is love and enjoyment.
Enjoying ourselves and doing the things we love to do
Being with the people we love being with
Laughing, singing
Having fun . . .

. . . We are in touch with ourselves when we are living a life of ease,
acknowledging the love, happiness, prosperity,
health and beauty that we are,
and being truly generous with
ourselves . . .

When we are truly generous with ourselves, others are
truly generous with us.
First we must acknowledge the Divinity that we are before
others will acknowledge us.
They can now see It in us, and we can see It in them.
In being good to ourselves, we are opening the way to our
greatest contribution to others.

. . . When love enters in, fear and self-condemnation
disappear . . .

HEAVEN IS NOW

"When I look to the past I am dying. When I look to the future I am dying. Life is now. I must know the life that IS."

When I ask a computer to give me information and solutions, it can only look into its programming to provide an answer.
It has nowhere else to look.
By its very nature a computer must look into the past.
The same is true of the mind.
When I look with the mind, I see only the past.
When I look at a flower, an animal or a problem I am facing, the mind searches for information, stacked in multi-sensory records from the past, through which I can comprehend an experience.
It can do nothing else.
When I want to project a future, the mind looks once again in the past for information, through which it makes its projection.

. . . I am left with a lot of past and a lot of future; a lot of beliefs and a lot of opinions; and I know they are all illusions and have no existence other than those my mind gives them . . .

I know that when I live in the mind and operate from there, I see a confusing world.
I see good and bad and health and disease.
I see struggle and effort and lack and need.
Life is a prison, a battleground, meaningless, fear-ridden.
I don't understand it, I can't find my place, and nothing really makes any sense.
And then there's God and devil and light and shadow and a million beliefs about this and that.

. . . And none of it has anything to do with the Now . . .

This is the human condition, the belief that I have an identity separate from Self, the belief that I am a mind/body complex.
This is the belief that brings all the misery and struggle.
I can unshackle my attachment to these beliefs.

. . . And the less the reality of past and future, and all dualities, the more I am at peace in eternity, which is not a length of time, but right now in this very moment . . .

In order to unshackle the past it is first necessary to want to unshackle it, secondly to know that it is binding me, and thirdly to be willing to do the work to liberate myself.
I find that the past dissolves when Self is present, just as shadow disappears when light is present.
Shadow has no reality when Self is present, nor have any of the so-called problems of the world.
When Life is present how can there be death?
When Love is present how can there be hate?
When God is present how can there be devil?

. . . When One is present how can there be two? . . .

Alignment with Self is the key: in remembering that, I find myself.
In true prayer and meditation the Self is revealed as infinite Space containing all.

. . . Unconditional Love knows no judgements, and is a presence that has no solutions, but by its very nature is all solutions . . .

Suddenly Heaven becomes here and now and not a far off place.
Life becomes immortal by the very fact that I am alive; and the world becomes perfect just the way it is.
Freedom comes when I surrender a belief in the power of evil.
Struggling ceases when I give up my puny attempts to manipulate the world to suit my mind, and my mind-created problems disappear just as if they are ice-cubes dissolving in the warmth of the ocean of Love and mercy.

When Self is present vision returns, a vision clear of the hindrances of history and duality, and I can see things as they really are.

. . . I can heal my universe, dwell in the world of the wondrous, and create a heaven here and now . . .

THE SOUND CURRENT

We are often preparing for something—like musicians practising—even for when we can live . . . waiting until we are qualified.

Some people get to ninety without having the qualifications.
Better to know that *this* is life, and to live it now.
If you want to put yourself into a training programme *while* living, that is a better approach, but don't practise for it.

. . . You have all the capacities and all the skills, by the very fact that you exist in nature, by the very fact that you *are*
By the fact that you are the sound current in operation . . .

The sound current is the very source of life.
It is who we are.
We don't need to tune into it, because we are it.
We only need to express it, in many different ways, through our voice or our actions.

Every electrical movement in the system, in the body
and in the universe is the sound current in
action.
This is an electrical universe which is trying to find a
harmony in its opposites.
The positive and negative electrical impulses, the two
aspects of the sound current, are trying to come into
harmony.

. . . Everything which is happening in life is an attempt to
come into harmony with the sound current . . .

What is happening in your life, the negative and positive,
which you might describe as bad and good, is only the
two polarities trying to find a unity.
There is only the One.
Always come back to "I am It".
Forget "Becoming It".
Ignore "If you do this and that, you're OK".

. . . You are already there . . .

The will is the ability to hold our vision.
Most people think of willpower as force.
Force is a natural force, but not a force over others.
The true force is our state of being, which is able to
transform another person.
Most people's force is used to gain power over others, so
that they can "look better".
The extent to which we allow people to have power over
us is the extent to which we die.

. . . We are all individual free cells.
Nothing has power over a cell of your body.
It lives and has its life by itself . . .

It is an independent free cell, which lives in harmony with other cells.
If it didn't, it would be in trouble.
The same for us.
We can live as an individual, sourceful being, in harmony with all other cells, knowing that we're sourced by the same thing, all equal, all with our separate purposes, just as the cells in our body (brain, fingers, hair) have different functions but are all equal.
We can make the connection between the cells of this system and the cells of the universal system.
We can see how the world is going to move.

At the moment the world functions in a forced system.
It wants to come into harmony with the natural system, which means freedom of individuals—individuals in alignment with one another, recognising the common Source.

People talk about the light and the sound.
They are actually the same.
We cannot separate the light and the sound.
Think of light being the light of awareness, of knowledge, the light of understanding.
Knowledge is then considered to be the light.
The power to produce is considered as the sound current.
Unless we're in touch with the sound current, unless we can produce, what is the use of the knowledge?
Tremendous knowledge, which we are in no way able to produce in the world, is of no value.
It's nice to know so much, but it has no real value.
If you have the power to produce from this knowledge, then you have the sound current.

. . . The sound current might be defined as "the pillar of Who We Are, which empowers us to produce" . . .

We come into life by the application of the sound current.
We transmit it by our voice and thinking.
The way we get in touch with it more is by being in tune with ourselves.

If you speak with power, then what you speak is true.
This is the real power of the spoken word.
If you speak with doubt, it does not have the same power, and will not manifest.
There are people who have developed to the point that they can say, "Get up and be healed" and the patient is healed.
The power of the current, with no doubt attached to it, is the power of manifestation.
That which creates in the universe is the sound current.
As we begin to be more in touch with it and master it in the physical world, we can demonstrate joy, health, happiness, love, wealth, or whatever it is we wish to demonstrate into the world.
This we do by the very fact of our speaking and our thinking, but not by "thinking about".

. . . Creative thinking is applying the power of the sound current . . .

The light and the sound come from the same source: there is only one Source, the God Source.
"In the beginning was the word" (sound current).
"I am the word."
The more we get in tune with that, the more we have power to express in life.

. . . Beware of misinterpretations of the Christian religion which don't allow you to be the word . . .

Don't try to escape the physical world: that type of thinking is a cul-de-sac.

We have to find the heights and then come down and transform the depths.
Our opportunity is to take our awareness and use it to spiritualise or transform the physical world.
There are classic examples of 'spiritual seekers' who spend a lot of their time getting out of their bodies into a higher dimension, and yet whose lives are a mess.

...Denying the physical world is denying a part of God. Own the world, both material and spiritual...

Working in consciousness is the only thing really worth doing.
Money is a dramatically demonstrable spiritual form: there is so much energy around it.
For many people money is "Who I am"; they can't transform it into love.
God and love are everything; therefore they must be money as well.
A German student of mine had cancer of the throat.
He had toured throughout the East, consulting one guru after another.
When asked by what principles he lived, he said, "There is only Love".
But he had not included his cancer in that Love.

...By changing his attitude to the cancer, he was able to change his whole situation.
Pain is the effort to deny God, or Love...

See everything as transformed into consciousness, even
disease and fear.
Our whole lives are an expression of the sound current.
When you chant, your whole being resonates the sound,
which reaches out to others.

. . . You don't have to *do* anything to be the sound current.
You don't have to *be* anything to be all right.
Just so with loving . . .

TRANSFORMING RELATIONSHIPS

Strangers are friends we have not yet met.
We are exploring relationships and transformation of relationships.

The 1980's were the decade of communication and information.
There was a massive growth in the communication of information and with it a growth in the communication between human beings.
In the 1980's work in the development of awareness was substantially in the area of communication, one with another.
Learning to tell the truth, learning to take responsibility, learning to let go the barriers to being.

. . . The shift is in learning to cooperate with each other, rather than be in conflict.
We see this happening in our personal relationships and at a national and global level . . .

The 1990's *are the age of transformation.*
Communication and information are head activities . . .
Transformation is to do with the heart.
This age is about relationships, opening the heart, giving and receiving.
In relationships now, people think in terms of a "you" and a "me".
We are striving in some ways to get these bodies together.
The difficulty of this is that our bodies represent only a small part of our total being.
What is unseen is a massive amount of baggage, incomplete relationships from the past, which we now bring to the present one.

. . . When we think that we are only a form, a body, relating becomes effort, struggle and pain . . .

When I bring my baggage to a relationship, I am bringing all the things I am thinking consciously or subconsciously about my mother, father, sisters, brothers, my fears, jealousies, resentments, all the beliefs I have about myself and you, and all the people you remind me of.
I then say, "Let's have a relationship!"
This relationship has about a 5% chance of being nourishing, as the rest of us is taken up in all the other relationships.
We probably have a lot of 5% relationships.
By "incomplete" what I mean is I have thinking and feeling about you other than love, goodwill and gratitude.

...In a complete relationship, whenever I think of you, I feel love, goodwill and gratitude and have no sense of separation from you...

We are revealing that "love alone is".
We think that we relate to this person or that person, but in fact they are reflecting back to us, or reminding us, of past relationships that are incomplete.
Love IS,—it's not a form or a thing.
We are not looking for ways in which bodies can relate to bodies.
That thinking leads to loneliness and pain.
We are talking about love—love that seeks itself and seeks to express itself.

...There is nothing we have to do in order to have love.
We just have to UNdo the thinking that stands in the way.
We reverse the process...

Trying to make our relationships work is hardly likely to succeed.

The more we try, the more we struggle, the more we stifle the truth.
Everybody on the planet is a brother and sister in spirit.
They are all friends we have not yet met.
How is it that we treat them as enemies?
We can change our thinking.

. . . Instead of me trying to relate to you, I can acknowledge that I am *already* in relationship with you.
Relationship becomes a context of being . . .

That changes our perspective.
"In relationship" with you is like saying I am "in the swimming pool" with you or "in the room" with you.
The swimming pool and the room are the context "Relationship within which we are".
We do not have to forge a relationship; we are already in it.

. . . Now it is simply a matter of discovering the truth of our relationship, whether we are friends, partners. lovers, or simply fellow human beings . . .

In discovering who we are, we discover the truth of our relationship.
In knowing who I am, I know who you are.

. . . In knowing who you are, I can relate to you as you are, *and* to who you think you are.
I can also relate from "who I am", and not from "who I think I am." . . .

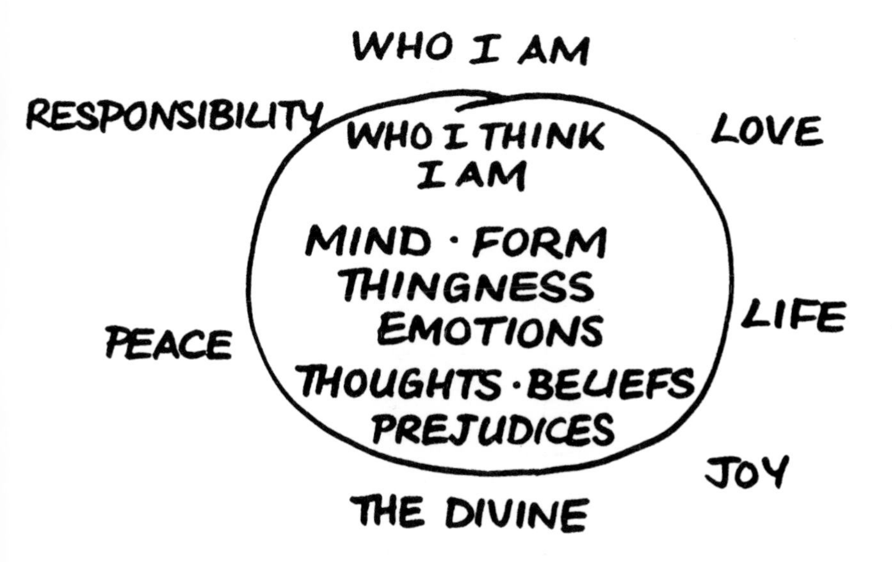

Outside the circle is beingness, and that is who I am.
Beingness is not a form, not a thing.
It is space.
And as we release our formbound thinking, we have a new perspective.

The moment we notice, observe, are alert to or aware of the thinking that we have and the feelings that come up, we know that we are not these.
We are that which contains it.
That which contains this body contains all bodies and is all bodies.

Inside the circle are thoughts, feelings and form.
Blame, jealousy and burden live inside the circle.
When we live life from inside the circle, we blame people.
When we live outside the circle, we take responsibility for whatever we are thinking and feeling.
Until I recognise that I am Love and you are Love, there are merely some errors in my thinking to correct.
To do this I recognise I am the wholeness that contains and permeates all thinking, feeling and bodies.
When I believe I am my mind, body and feelings, when pain arises, I must place the blame somewhere.
I blame you for what you did to me or what you didn't do to me and I manipulate you, control you and compete with you.
It is like saying, "I'm the air" and I notice that in the air there are many bodies.

When people protest that a loved one spurns them, ask the question, "Where do we experience love?"
Is my experience of love in another body, somewhere over there?
Do the test: where DO you experience love?
Does it not happen in our own heart?
Is it not an experience of "over here"?
Could it not be that we just close down to the experience of love and blame another?
Other people reflect our own love.

. . . Love doesn't go anywhere.
Love is not a form.
We simply close down to it . . .

What is the mechanism of jealousy?
It is a belief that my love exists over there, in that body that I pin it on, and someone has taken what is mine.
It is a denial of the truth which is, "I am the source of love and no one can take love from me."
I can, however, close myself to it.

The key to transformation is to free the body and every cell in it from stone-age thinking patterns.
The way to transform our relationships in the area of jealousy is to acknowledge that I am the source of my love.
If I am the source and I want love in my life, the key is to go out and love.
What we give we receive.
When we go out and love people, it comes flooding back.
Jealousy ends and we have lots of love in our life.

. . . Go to the vulnerable state of totally giving of yourself. That is what commitment is . . .

What of resentment?
The word resentment comes from the French for "re-feel".
Resentment is re-feeling a past upset.
Every time I see you or think of you I re-feel the pain I think I am in.
These feelings are in my body.

. . . *The liberation from these feelings comes through consciously refeeling our emotions and returning them to love and light.*
In love, we free ourselves from all the thoughts and feelings we're clinging to.
Everything that is in the way of love is re-experienced and dissolved.
This process returns us to health, happiness, prosperity and well-being . . .

It is the effort we are making to hold on to negative thoughts and feelings that creates and recreates the pain that we feel.
Everything that we hold on to adds to the pain in the universe.
We can refeel it unconsciously and apportion blame, or we can refeel it consciously and responsibly and release ourselves from the past hurt.
This is the process of forgiveness—to "give for", or give up our attitudes that stand in the way of love.
Other people are not the source of our pain; they merely mirror the pain we are already in.
As such they are a gift to us, if we can see it that way.

. . . Behind every problem is a gift—look for it . . .

Problems give us an opportunity to bring up and dissolve our unconscious resistances to love.
You know when you have released the pain; you feel good about that person again.
You can either re-feel it, or you can release the past hurt.
The proof of the pudding is when love and goodwill return.
I am not speaking about sentimentality.
I'm talking about a love that is unbound, free and permanent.

Grief is the belief that I am separated from my love.
When we think love is a form, grief arises—and separation comes.

When we relate to the essence of all people, and know that at that level we are one with them, no separation occurs on the death of the body.
The pain we feel need only be short-lived, merely the loss of a friend in a physical sense.
The love and the essence live on in the cells of your own body.
This is very important to know when we lose a parent, partner, child, or other loved one.
They have gone nowhere.
They are still here.
Their total being lives on.

. . . Death is something that lives in the mind. Reincarnation lives there, too . . .

The fear of being left by a loved one can often be the barrier to entering into marriage.
If, for example, a woman lost her father when she was a young girl, it's quite possible that she takes on the belief that "those whom I love die".
A subconscious resistance to marriage will then arise for fear that her partner will die, as she loves him.
She thinks it is better not to give herself rather than to face that possibility.
She will also always tend to look for her father in a relationship, as that fundamental relationship is not healed.

. . . The key in this instance is to surrender the father in love and heal the belief in separation . . .

Family thinking patterns and actions constantly repeat themselves, unless changed in consciousness.
An abused child tends to abuse his or her children.
That which was done to us we do to others.
Incompletions pass from parent to child.

The sins of the father (and mother) are visited on the child.
At the age of about two and a half, we take on personality.
Personality is the dungeon of life.
Personality robs us of joy.

. . . You don't need personality training; just be yourself . . .

"Sinning" means missing the mark, our patterns which hold us from love.
When we recognise the patterns and bring them consciously into the light of awareness, we can dissolve and change them.
Maybe your father would never touch anybody—he was not at all tactile.
Now you find that you are that way with your children or the people you are trying to relate to.
By acknowledging that you are not your father—you are love—you are free to love the way that suits you and that you find nourishing.

. . . When we heal the limiting patterns, greater joy and happiness arise . . .

People say, "I need love".
Need is not the way to get what you want, whether it's love, money, success or whatever.

The message 'I need love' comes from the belief that I am not love and that "my love is over there".
In the needing you rob yourself of it.
It runs away, as you probably know.
The truth is that we are the source of love.
Rather than needing love, go out and love.
When upset or hurt, rather than wallowing in it, ask "Who can I reach out to? Who calls for my help?"

. . . Pick up the phone and talk to someone,—reach out, and you will find your need disappears.
This is the fastest way out of it . . .

The greatest fear is the fear of love.
Nutty, but true.
If I say to you, "How good are you willing to have it? How much love, joy, fun, sex and money do you want?" what is your reply?
You will probably say, "Lots of it!". But look into your thinking.
Look at all those mind patterns which are there saying, "I *shouldn't* really have it. In some way it's wrong."
The fear to have what you *really* want, which is a life full of everything wonderful, robs you.

. . . The Bible says it is the Father's good pleasure to give you the Kingdom. Not just a little now and then, but *everything* I have is yours.
Accept the gift . . .

My thinking and feelings are giving me the messages—my body is the transformer.
We can transform all the ugly into beautiful, all the pain into joy,
All the sickness into health, and the death into life.
We are the transformers.
We are the leaders.

We are the people who are going to take the planet to its next level.
We are those who acknowledge the quantum leap that is available,—and make it known.
Every time we raise our consciousness a little bit, we do it for everybody.

. . . We are interrelated; we are not separate . . .

Attempting to hold your life together with effort or attempting to manipulate people to give you what you think you need leads to stress and doesn't work.
We have no need to hold the stars together.
There is a natural order in things.
When we are willing to trust, our lives naturally fall into place and far greater riches emerge than those our limited thinking tried to force.

Just relax, trust and know that that which is truly for you,—endless gifts of love and joy—comes to you in peace and stillness.
They are already yours and always were.
We are learning to give and receive love.
Love is yours already.
All you have to do is let go of whatever or whoever it is you are holding onto.
You find naturally and spontaneously that you begin to feel good about yourself and about other people.

Attraction for many people begins to arise.
You find feelings of love arise with many others.
When you are attracted, move towards the attraction—but move towards it with integrity.
You will find there is a gift there for you.
As you move into love with someone, you find your partner has a sudden expansion of love and takes on the characteristics of the attraction you felt.

If, for example, you were attracted to someone's aliveness and you move towards this with integrity in your own relationship, the gift of aliveness you receive from this attraction is bestowed upon you, your partner, and everybody in your consciousness.

. . . What you have fallen in love with is Love.
Just acknowledge that; that is what lifts you . . .

That which is real cannot disappear.
Love cannot disappear.
That which is unreal disappears in love.
The cloud that is in the way vanishes.

HEALING FAMILY KARMA

Karma means unfinished business, something that is not resolved.
It means something that has to be completed in order that Love, well-being, and the truth of being are present.

We can see in our past and throughout our daily life that there are certain things that we need to resolve.
They are unfinished and incomplete.
When we discover that this is true, we can call it our karma.
Often it is described as something heavy—a burden.

. . . Think of it as something joyful, fun and really worth doing.
It is the process of living itself . . .

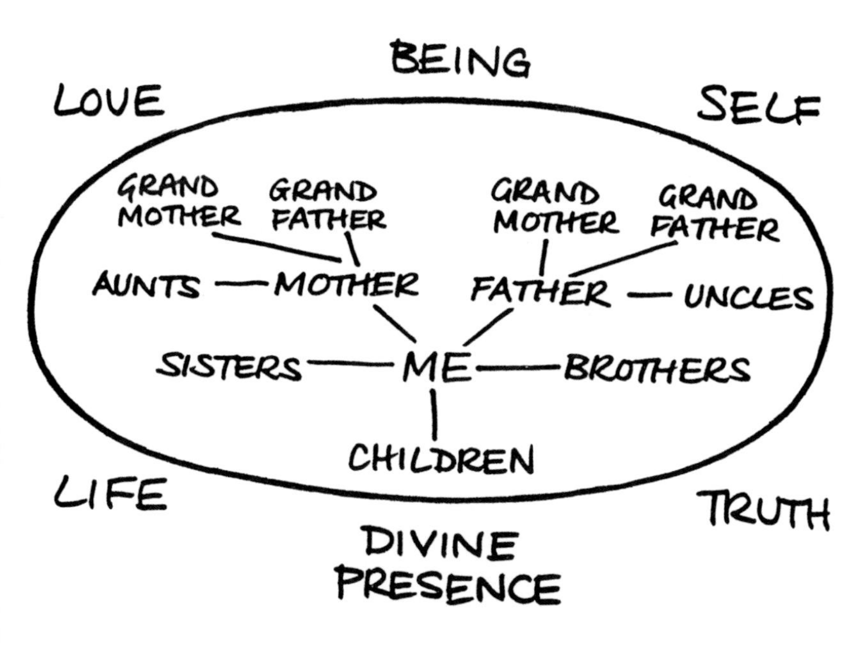

The circle contains all the people who are a part of your family.

You are at the centre, then your parents, then four grandparents, various brothers and sisters, husband, wife and children.

There may be others in your map—the people who were important to you in your growing up phase, particularly in the first eight years of your life.

Include aunts, uncles, godparents, friends of your father's or mother's who have had a significant influence on your life.

Also include ex-spouses, boy/girlfriends and ex-lovers.

Similar maps can be drawn for your partner and children.

Why did you choose your partner?

. . . What is the Karma to be resolved in the relationship? What are the gifts you bring to each other? . . .

Your particular family is very important for you.
You chose it. It is a substantial part of your journey to freedom, peace, love, joy, in fact 'Home'.
We are often taught to ignore or to rise above the family—not to be involved and not to be a part of it.
Certain disciplines try to cut you off from your family, make you turn away from it.
That doesn't work, because your family resides in you.
It is not a thing.
It is a state of consciousness.
You can't escape it.
Everything in the map is very relevant to each of us.

. . . Each part of the family that is unresolved is a part of ourselves unresolved..
When you look from the vision of Oneness, Love and Being, each person in the family is there working to help you complete your life, to become the Source.
Source, Love, Life are all outside the circle and have no form.
It is the space of Being.
When we have found the truth of Being and Love, the whole family becomes a contribution to our next level of existence.
That level is resolving the karma of a particular group of people, country or religion.

. . . Ultimately we talk about resolving all the Karma on the planet . . .

That is an opportunity to grow, to transform and not a problem.
In treating this as joyful work, we bring about the transformation of the mental, emotional and physical world in stages.
'Family problems' become 'family opportunities' or 'family gifts'.
Instead of saying "I have family problems", say, "What are the gifts that my family are presenting to me?" "What opportunities?"

The whole family is contained in Love, so that the basis of the family is love.
Often we see the family as a problem—unfinished business.
"I'm resentful towards a parent, angry with my father or upset with my mother."
If we look at it in this way—for instance rejection from a parent—we create a closing to the feeling of love.

So we chase around the world trying to find love.
We find that the unfinished business turns up in all our other relationships.
If I'm incomplete with my mother, I find myself distant in all the relationships I have with women.
If I feel hurt by my father, I find myself taking revenge in all my male relationships.
The extent to which we are incomplete with anyone in the family is the extent to which we are incomplete with others.
It is a good idea to start resolving it.

. . . Unless there is love and harmony in our relationships with all our family members, it will stand in the way of all our other relationships . . .

If I had a particular incompletion with my father, it is very likely he had the same one with his father, my grandfather with his father, and so on back through the generations.
If your mother has a particular incompletion with her father, she will probably have this same difficulty with your father.
If she is bitchy with you, it is quite probable that she had an incompletion with her mother or someone else further back in the family line.
What is done to her she does to her children.

. . . It is not a matter of genes, it is a matter of consciousness . . .

We carry a certain consciousness, a thinking pattern.
Until we see this pattern, unshackle and resolve it, it will continue down the generations.
"The sins of the father are visited on the son."
If my father feels he is a failure, I probably will, too, for no explainable reason and irrespective of how well I may appear to be doing. It passes down until we personally resolve it.
To heal that pattern I must return the belief or feeling to the Space, to Love.

The first step is, to recognise the limiting thought or feeling, in this case a sense of failure.
Second, be willing to give up the attitude that separates you from Love.
Unless you're willing, nothing can change.
Third, take responsibility: recognise that you placed the distance between you and the person you're complaining of, remember when you did it and for what reason.
You can see that you created the whole issue, so only you can heal it.

If you acknowledge that Love is the basis of all life, there is only happiness once everything is returned to Love.

Give up the negative attitude or emotion, but as if you were giving it back to the Divine, saying, "You can have this back. I accept only Love."
If you find difficulty in giving up the attitudes or feelings, ask inside for help.
If you still have difficulty, seek out someone skilled in this field to assist.

. . . You know when you have done it: there is a feeling of release and love floods into your being.
The pain goes . . .

Healing our relationships can be easy.
Give up TRYING to do it, give up the effort.
Not, "I've GOT to do it."
'Must' holds it away, whereas 'I ***am healing*** *my relationship with my mother' brings it about.*
'Must' means a future event, which I probably don't intend to do.
'I ***am****, or I* ***choose*** *to do it' opens it into a vision.*
See yourself doing it and it is easy.

Take inequality.
If I still look to my father as if he were older and superior, and I have to be a son to him even when I'm fifty years old, I haven't resolved my relationship.
He is still treating me fatherly and I'm still being a son.
How would my girlfriend take it if I'm always looking for a mother and not for an equal partner?
She would find it very irritating, unless she were looking for a little boy to mother in preference to having a whole relationship.
We have daughters being 'Daddy's little girl', men looking for little girls to look after or 'play Daddy' to, and infinite other variations.

. . . None of them are really satisfying—they are not equal, whole relationships . . .

Parents are the most important relationships in our life.
They are the people from whom we decide what relationship is like.
If I've had a lousy relationship with my mother, that's how I think women are.
Since 95% of us is unresolved, subconscious, we cannot deal with it until it is brought into the conscious mind.
So resolve your relationships with your parents because they are your major people.
The relationship they have with each other is how we judge marriage.

Go into your relationships with your parents—be the source, the centre.
From there you can heal the relationships backwards.
You bring the healing.
So the children come to heal the parents (if they choose to).
As we heal our past, backwards, we also heal forwards—our relationships with our children.

. . . We do the work for all of them . . .

You probably know that there are certain patterns that show up in your family,
Perhaps a certain illness, or alcoholism, or aggression, or even accidents.

If a great-grandfather dies at sea, the pattern often repeats itself.
The same may be true for motor accidents, or for family members who die at a certain age.
Sometimes fear runs through a family.
Healing the family Karma is returning to love, to a love-based family, not fear-based.

... Transform all the energies into love.
Fear is unresolved love: an energy that is not yet transformed ...

When we are born, we walk into the family consciousness.
We choose it.
We have the family thinking for generations: religious, social, political, ethnic, national, educational and professional.
In a military family, "Unless I'm battle-scarred, I'm not doing very well!"
A church family might impose, "Unless you're fighting the devil, you are slacking."
You don't have to renounce the thinking, but recognise it for what it is.
Jewish thinking is like this, Christian like this.
I'm still a free, loving being.

On top of the thinking pattern I'm born into, I make some decisions from birth about whether people love me or not, whether I'm good or not good, wanted or not wanted.
The mind is like a computer programme.
By the time I'm eight, I have my thinking full up. The computer is almost fully established. Everything after that becomes just a reflection, a comparison with my formative thinking—unless I consciously work to change that thinking.

If we can see that we are not our thinking, but Being looking through thinking, we can hold out the whole thinking structure and see what is useful or not in it.

. . . All that is love-based is useful—the rest we should transform . . .

Even if a parent or other family member has died, we can still heal our relationships with them.
I heal my relationship with someone in my own consciousness.
If I have got something going on about someone who has died—grief, anger or upset—I heal it here, in consciousness.
The principle works just the same: bring them to mind, see what it is in the space (whether grief, anger or upset), give up your attitude, acknowledge the divinity, knowing that they haven't gone anywhere.
If you really think about death, the wonderful thing is that all they have given up is their thinking patterns.

. . . They are still present; they have just let go of the form . . .

Think about that: if you truly are with someone who dies consciously, or if somebody in your family dies and you are truly in Love with them, a transformation occurs. The negative and limited thinking which they give up resolves in you, because there is no separation. You do the same for them.
Death becomes something joyful and beautiful, not a tragedy.
If someone dear to you has died, that is a most beautiful gift to you; it has given you the gift of love, the gift of freedom, providing you return it to Love.

. . . It has given you the opportunity to resolve consciously all the patterns that they were holding on to.
They resolve in you.
If we can truly get that, it is a wonderful experience . . .

If you have a parent or a child who died, the gift is a gift of love.
Someone who was grieving over her daughter who had died realised that if she truly saw the gift of her death, she would find that her daughter would show up in every daughter.
Wherever she saw 'daughter', that child would also be hers.

Another person, who was in deep misery over the death of her husband, recognised that, now she had given up his body, he lived in her heart.
If she loved from the heart, she received the gift of love and would find him in all men.
So she would feel more loving to all men, and her husband would reflect in all men to her.
Once she began to see it that way, she realised she had not lost something.
She had gained a tremendous gift.

Of course, we feel sad in the physical sense, because that person who was close to us isn't here.
But if we know that this sadness becomes joy and love, and that there is no error in anything, then it is all a part of the gift that person has given us.

. . . Acknowledge people, your family, your friends, everyone for the gift they are to you . . .

Responsibility leads to forgiveness and gratitude, the two pillars of healing.

When we can be grateful to each other for the gifts that are brought, we can begin to see the tremendous beauty of our family.
A difficult family becomes an Aladdin's cave of treasures yet to be found.
Healing the family is something we do in ourselves.
Don't rush home to your family saying, "I've found out what's wrong with you all. You've now got to change!"
There is no one we have to change except ourselves.

. . . If the work is truly done the others will follow.
Love is contagious . . .

Each of us becomes our own sun—our own opportunity, our own way of completing the relationships.
And each of us alone is the one who returns all to Love . . .

INDIVIDUALS MATTER

It takes each of us to create the condition of the planet as it now is.
It will take each of us to transform this condition.

Do you want to be maimed or killed in a war?
Do you want people to starve to death in their millions unnecessarily?
Do you want to be sick and in pain, penniless and discarded?
It would be a stupid person who said yes to these questions.
So why do these conditions persist when only madmen want them?
On the surface the answer seems to be that people believe that certain conditions are inevitable and there is nothing they can do about them.

I hear people say, "There will always be war. This is a warring universe", or, "We will always have death by starvation. It is just one of the unfortunate facts of life."
"If things are inevitable, why try to do something about it?" people say, "It is a waste of energy and achieves nothing.
You might as well go unconscious and forget about it."
This is the condition we find ourselves in.

What is the lie here?
The lie is that individuals don't matter, that individuals don't make a difference.

The lie is rooted in the belief that each of us is a separate microcosmic unit of a body and a mind.
We identify with this body/mind unit and see our helplessness in the seeming vastness of the problem.
From this viewpoint the statement, "There is nothing I can do" is accurate.

. . . The human self, by itself, is helpless, like a blaring radio stuck on one channel with no one to turn the knobs . . .

The truth is individuals *do* make a difference.
When the individual knows he or she is the Source and returns to that awareness, everything becomes possible and what hitherto has never been done can now be done.
It is not activity on the mind side that brings the change, but individuals returning to Source.

. . . It is up to us.
Each of us . . .

The starting place is in our own consciousness.
Until we have cleared the debris of past attitudes and attachments from the pure stream of consciousness, we can do little that is useful to assist others.

. . . Until that time, 'helping' can be 'hindrance and interference' . . .

Until we can see clearly, we tend to blame life and the people we see in it for our unhappy circumstances, rather than acknowledging our own self-created drama and using the experience with gratitude to move us nearer the Source.

Once we have ceased to identify with the mind and body as 'Who we are' and realign with the Soul Self (or an awareness of 'I Am'), the possibilities and the opportunities flood into consciousness.
Vision returns and we are able to see life and the world in a way that we may never have seen them, or may not have dared to since childhood.

. . . What some may call "mere dreams" or "flights of fancy" become possible and, if we engage in making them so, can become reality . . .

Landing on the moon was a dream and, at the time J. F. Kennedy announced the programme, it was also deemed by experts to be impossible.
Nevertheless, Kennedy's vision became reality because he took a stand that, not only *could* it be done, it *would* be done (even though no solution existed at that time).
Running a four-minute mile was "impossible" until Roger Bannister did it.
Now many athletes do it.
A hundred years ago flying across the English Channel was impossible and maybe inconceivable.
Now flying is a natural part of our daily lives.

These achievements come about because individuals aligned with Source, took a stand and generated the will to make them happen.

They happened because someone created the context or matrix within which the result could show up.
Once the idea of a man on the moon existed in consciousness, it was only a matter of time before someone took responsibility for making it happen.

. . . Once the idea of flight was born, a group of determined people brought the idea into form . . .

It was not governments or organisations or institutions or experts that brought these things into existence.
It was individuals like you and me.
In the first instance it was not vast numbers of people that brought the change.
It was one or two people saying, "It can be done for no other reason than because I say so."

Bob Geldof of Live Aid put on a concert in aid of the starving that reached over a billion people.
It had never been done before, but one man did it.
Douglas Bader was told he could never walk without sticks, but he did, because he said he would.

. . . Every day, things are being done by ordinary people, which the experts deem impossible . . .

Looking at the present conditions of the world and of our lives, what seems inevitable?
What seems impossible?
Let us ask the question, "What do we really want?"
What are the opportunities available, however impossible they seem to us, to make our visions a reality?

. . . Can we look forward to a three-minute mile, the end of death by starvation, the elimination of cancer, peace on earth, personal enlightenment, the rule of spirit in our lives,?

Can we look forward to *your* personal vision becoming a reality? . . .

Participate in life in such a way that the conditions that we see are spiritualised.
Unwanted matter and forms are returned to the source.
In learning from them we release them, or transform them into something useful.
In this way the planet evolves through our creative participation.
In taking this responsibility, we transform the conditions which are destroying the planet, and create whole new possibilities, many of which have not even been thought of yet.
There is an urge, an opportunity, in East and West and North and South, to return to the Source, the silent centre within.

INTERDEPENDENCE

The more we explore within, the more we find that we are the greatest resource there is.

There's no consciousness or power external to us.
There's nothing or no one who is senior to us when we work from this expanded state of being.
We *are* the key to everything in our life.
No one can do it for us.
No one should do it for us.

In a dependent mode, such as being a child or being in hospital, there is a dependency, but only as part of the process.
Responsibility continues.
With responsibility, the seeds of our sovereignty lie within our 'dependency'.
We find ourselves as sovereign beings working with other sovereign beings.
We recognise that we are not dependent or independent, but interdependent.
We cannot do without each other.
We're all atoms in the same body.

Doing something of a damaging nature to *any* being, is damaging to us.
It is like cutting off a finger.

. . . Each person becomes a cell in our global body. The personal and the global can no longer be separated . . .

See the Oneness as a space.
It has no form.
It is not a thing.
In the space, 'thingness' thinking gives way.
Take all human beings and tie them together, and do you get 'human being', or do you simply have every human being tied together?
'Human beingness' is superior to the form 'human being'.
It is the space within which all human beings manifest.

We are human beingness.
We meet at the base of the iceberg.
We are human beingness expressing as this human being and that human being.
We are the microcosm and the macrocosm at the same time.
We are totally interdependent and interrelated.
Why see others as strangers?
Why be afraid of other cells of your own body?

. . . Everyone becomes a friend we've not yet met, a cell of our own body we've not yet owned . . .

BEYOND GOOD AND EVIL

To me the major problem that remains unresolved in the world is the belief in the existence of two powers, good and evil.
All crises and conflicts are an attachment to this belief.

As we look around, we observe many examples of good and evil at work.
There are good people and evil people, good ideas and evil ideas, good forces and evil forces.
As we observe them they have a definite reality.
They are not imagination as we are sometimes asked to believe.
If we bury our heads in the sand they won't go away.

. . . There are definitely dark forces and there are definitely evil people.
Or are there? . . .

At one level this is true.
It is obvious and demonstrable and we can see it all around us.

But if we look from another perspective, things change a little.
Let us look for a moment from the viewpoint of the great mystics
and teachers who all say in their own words there is only the One, the One God, the One Self, the One Power.
This is telling us that from where they look, there are not two powers or ten powers, but only one power and *that* power has all the attributes of God: goodness, wholeness, prosperity, love, joy and freedom to name a few.

... So where did we get the notion there are two powers? Good and evil, right and wrong, peace and war, God and devil? ...

For an answer to this question we must understand the nature of the mind.
The mind, like the computer, is dualistic in nature.
It can only operate in a dualistic way and thus it creates a world of opposites.
It must think in terms of love and hate, health and disease, life and death.
It knows no other way and cannot see beyond itself.
If we align ourselves with mind this is the only reality we have.
As mind-oriented beings, if we try to be good, we must create bad, if we strive for peace we must create war, if we have some mental concept of God we must create a devil.
All of these are balancing powers which we create out of mind.
They go hand in hand.

... There is another way ...

We can align ourselves with the Soul Self, the Self which is beyond polarities.
We can recognise that the true Self is not the mind which separates us, but the Godself in which we are one.

. . . If we live in the Godself then we can neutralise the conflicts in our lives and dissolve the sense of separateness from the Source . . .

Let us look further at this thing called evil.
I have suggested it has a reality in a mind-oriented existence and is the opposite aspect of the mind interpretation of good.
It is also interesting that the word 'live' spelt backwards is 'evil' (and 'devil' contains the same word).
This may be coincidental or it may be that our wise ancestors considered anything that separated us from a full life, namely concepts of mind that limit our knowledge of our true selves, to be evil.
So that which stops us from being totally alive is evil, or that which suggests or induces death (once again a condition only known to the mind) is evil.

. . . Soul beyond polarities is immortal, whole, prosperous, living, healthy and free in eternity . . .

If evil exists only in the mind, then who is it who decides what is good and what is evil?
The answer must be, "I do".
I must decide for myself what is right and wrong and you must decide for yourself.
We look into our experience and upbringing and make decisions as to what is good and what is bad and then attach ourselves to these concepts as if they are *us*, and our existence depends on defending them.

. . . What we fail to notice is that other people have totally different ideas of right and wrong and they think *we* need correction! . . .

This is where the problem begins.
If I think I'm right, I must think you are wrong, unless you agree with me.
If you don't agree with me, we are heading for an argument and a breakdown in our relationship.
Even if you do agree with me it isn't much better.
We can win a few friends over to our point of view, but then we are bound to meet the same number of people (or the same strength of influence) who think we are wrong and the result is a strike or a war.
The mind with its attachments to viewpoints or positions creates the havoc that exists at all levels of life.

. . . The mind has no solutions to the problems it initiates and to look in the mind for solutions is a waste of time . . .

So what is the function of mind?
It is a necessary instrument for us to have existence here, and can act as a valuable servant or vehicle through which spirit can operate, but it is not who we are.
We are not that.
We are not ants on a huge flying rock groveling for crumbs.
Not in our true Selves.
We are princes and princesses in the kingdom of God with total ownership, unlimited and free.
To realise this, to experience it as a reality, rather than a nice idea we don't fully believe (but hope is true), we must be beyond the polarities of mind and dwell in the Soul plane of true Being, that place where there is no loneliness.
The mind must surrender.

I observe in my life that the mind does not want to surrender.
It is having far too much of a good time running things, however dismally they turn out.
It is afraid that if it surrenders, especially to a power it knows little or nothing about (though it has lots of good concepts of what it is), it will lose control, disappear, be annihilated.
It struggles hard to hang on.
It doesn't want to die.
Yet it is the surrender of the mind to the Godself that brings the moments of illumination, healing, love, and joy that thrill the mind and enthuse it in a manner beyond anything it can produce itself.

One solution is to go into a place of quiet a few times a day for ten minutes or half an hour and 'allow' the Inner Presence (some call it the Inner Master): that which knows all, heals, loves, and dissolves conflict to flow into my consciousness and into my life.
Any evil which I am experiencing is dissolved in this Healing Presence, as is doubt, fear, and the whole multitude of needs and wants.

I discover I am the infinite space, I am the nothingness, and I am the 'everythingness'.
I contain the whole.
Space and time become something within me.
They become constructions I create within which to express in this world.

...In these moments, knowing the Master, the mind is happy to be the servant...

In meditation we experience Being
Being is the state of who we *are*.
It has no limitation.

It has no structure.
It has no personality.

If each of us could find some time each day to dwell in the Godself, to dissolve that which troubles us and make the same opportunity available to others, we would all experience as true, beyond any questions or doubts, that we are of the same Source, one with each other, and that it is only our mental attachments that separate us.
When we do this, the fundamental problem of the world disappears.

There is the story of God wanting a holiday:
He calls together the three wisest men on the planet.
He says, "I'm so tired of people praying to me and wanting things, that I wish to take a holiday. I don't know where to go, but I want to go somewhere where *no one* is going to find me."
The first wise man says, "Go to the top of Everest, no one will find you there."
God replies, "No, someone, someday, will come along with an ice axe and find me."
The second wise man says, "The bottom of the ocean! Take your holiday there."
He answers, "No, some chap in a deep sea submarine will come along and find me."
The third one says, "What about the moon? *No one* will find you there."
He replies, "An astronaut will find me there one day. I can't risk a holiday on the moon."
"I've got a much better idea. I'll take my holiday by hiding *in* everybody." Says God, "They're *not* going to look for me there. The very last place they're going to look for me is in themselves."